COLLEGE BUSINESS ENGLISH

JACK S. ROMINE

Oakland City College
Oakland, California

Englewood Cliffs, N.J. **PRENTICE-HALL, INC.**

PRENTICE-HALL INTERNATIONAL, INC., LONDON
PRENTICE-HALL OF AUSTRALIA, PTY., LTD., SYDNEY
PRENTICE-HALL OF CANADA, LTD., TORONTO
PRENTICE-HALL OF INDIA (PRIVATE) LTD., NEW DELHI
PRENTICE-HALL OF JAPAN, INC., TOKYO

Current printing (last digit):

13 12 11 10 9 8 7 6

LIBRARY OF CONGRESS CATALOG CARD NO.: 63-13275

PRINTED IN THE UNITED STATES OF AMERICA
C 14197

TO
THE
STUDENT

A PATTERN FOR SUCCESS

The modern business world depends on clear communications. In every organization it is expected that all employees will be able to read and follow directions. In addition, there must also be people who take a more active role in communication: someone must write a letter, submit a report to the stockholders, edit a committee study, formulate company policy, and handle hundreds of other tasks through writing. Furthermore, this writing must be accomplished as a routine duty, usually within a time limit, and it must be neat and accurate enough to stand public inspection. Continual rewriting or retyping to correct mistakes means extra time, and wasted time means wasted salary—a most unprofitable way to run a business!

Employers are aware, increasingly, that young people entering business would perform more effectively—from application to advancement—with additional training in written communication. The aim of this book is therefore to increase your ability to move swiftly to your most productive level.

THE APPROACH

The philosophy of this book is not merely to teach you to recognize errors, though that may be a desirable by-product. A more worthwhile goal is to acquaint you with the formation and arrangement of words, to give a positive sense of sound sentence structure. The sequence of materials is planned for as much carry-over as possible from unit to unit. Each unit has drill sentences to be analyzed for weakness or error, but included also are drills giving you an opportunity to write your own sentences to prove your understanding of what you are learning. These do-it-yourself drills, calling for imitation of acceptable models, will give you a realistic index of your progress.

YOUR QUALIFICATIONS

Anyone of normal intelligence and adequate motivation can learn to write acceptably. Your maturity in deciding on a business career and your determination to work toward it are excellent character recommendations. Your native grasp of language, that serves you so well in ordinary conversation, is a much stronger asset than you may perhaps realize. In this book it is utilized whenever possible.

If we measure language on a percentage scale, you are probably not more than five per cent away from qualifying as an acceptable speaker. In language, however, that five per cent distinguishes the educated man from the uneducated one. Through unconscious, natural learning you have already approached sentence mastery. Through conscientious study you can identify and eliminate unacceptable expressions and gain a solid grounding in skills primarily related to writing—mature sentence structure, capitalization, and punctuation.

TABLE
OF
CONTENTS

1 THE ELEMENTS OF SENTENCE MASTERY

Basic to effective communication is a broad view of how words are arranged into thought units or sentences. Like any process that functions efficiently, the English language has an underlying organization. This control is supplied by what we will refer to as the elements of sentence construction.

First, there are the three basic sentence patterns, the typical word orders by which we join a subject (the thing being talked about) to a predicate (what is asserted about the subject):

| The young man | signed the check. |
| (subject) | (predicate) |

Notice how your alarm system would go off if the words were ordered in a different way: *The check signed the man, The signed check the man, The signed the check man,* etc.

Second, there are the parts of speech, words which act within a sentence to name, assert, modify, or connect. In the sentence we are building, the subject is *man,* a naming word, and the predicate is *signed the check,* an asserting word (*signed*) plus another naming word (*check*). In order to fill out this sentence, we can introduce other parts of speech, like this:

The young man immediately signed the check and left.

Young modifies *man* and *immediately* modifies *signed. And* connects the two asserting words, *signed* and *left.* Again, notice the importance of word order. *Young* and *and* could not occur in any other position, while *immediately* can be shifted to only one other position, after *check.* Now the sentence contains a basic sentence pattern as well as naming, asserting, modifying, and connecting words.

More modifiers and connectives could be inserted, of course, but writing a mature sentence will require adding word groups, the third kind of sentence elements:

The young man *in the tweed suit* signed the check and left.
   (A word group called a *prepositional phrase* modifies *man.*)

The young man signed the check and left *before we could protest.*
   (A word group called a *dependent clause* modifies *left.*)

The young man *wearing the hat* signed the check and left.
   (A word group called a *verbal phrase* modifies *man.*)

The young man, *a new employee,* signed the check and left.
   (A word group called an *appositive* renames or reidentifies *man.*)

Don't be misled. Not all sentences are so easily analyzed as these, though all sentences are made with the same elements. Much of the time we speak and write sentences containing many word groups:

> The young man *wearing the hat* signed the check and left, *walking hurriedly.*

> The young man *in the tweed suit* signed the check *which we offered him* and left *before we could congratulate him.*

Sometimes, even, one word group serves as a part of still another word group. This can occur because word groups, despite their length, function as parts of speech:

> The young man, *realizing that he had been given a bonus for his extra work,* signed the check and left.

> (The complete verbal phrase is *realizing that he had been given a bonus for his extra work;* in turn the verbal phrase contains a dependent clause, *that he had been given a bonus for his extra work,* which names what is being realized; and in its turn the dependent clause contains a prepositional phrase, *for his extra work,* which modifies *bonus.*)

As you go through the book, look back at this section from time to time and use it to gauge your learning. If it becomes increasingly clear to you, then you may give yourself a good progress report.

In the following section you are going to be given a quick review of the parts of speech so that you will be able to follow the instruction about sentence patterns, our first important objective. In subsequent sections you will be given full, detailed explanations of the parts of speech and word groups, but right now you need only enough insight to pick out the subject and predicate in a sentence.

A REVIEW
OF
THE PARTS
2 # OF SPEECH

The words which are used in a sentence to name, assert, modify, and connect are conventionally labeled the parts of speech. Normally they are identified by applying the definitions given below, though later in this book you will be shown how to identify them according to their position with regard to other words in a sentence.

NAMING WORDS

A *noun* names a person, place, thing, or quality:

A person: *Miss Smith* is a *typist.*
A place: The company originated in *Springfield,* a small *city* in *Missouri.*
A thing: The *typewriter* needs a new *ribbon.*
A quality: We admired her *courage.*

A *pronoun* substitutes for a noun; it refers indirectly to a person, place, thing, or quality:

A person: Mr. Hodges re-opened the account for *us* as soon as *he* could.
A place: Kansas City developed rapidly after *it* became a railroad center.
A thing: The room was remodeled, and *it* now contains three desks chosen for *their* wood finishes.
A quality: Friendliness was her watchword, and *it* won her many sales accounts.

ASSERTING WORDS

A *verb* asserts action, possession, or state of being (existence):

Action: The manager *straightened* his tie and *approached* the customer.
Possession: Charlotte *has* a cold.
State of Being: The hallway *is* drafty.

MODIFYING WORDS

An *adjective* describes or limits a noun or pronoun:

Description (What kind?): *black* ink, *believable* story, *credit* union, *discount* house
Limitation (Which one?): *your* turn, *this* card, *that* play, *whose* question
(How many?): *several* mistakes, *two* clerks, *one* advertisement, *ten* bids

An *adverb* limits the meaning of:

a verb: The order arrived *quickly.*
an adjective: The lawyer requested an *exceptionally* accurate typist.
another adverb: He spoke *very* softly.

Adverbs answer the questions *when? where? how?* and *to what degree?*

3

Time: You will be hired *soon.*
Place: Put the file cabinet *there.*
Manner: Accept the promotion *proudly.*
Degree: I invested an *unusually* large sum of money.

CONNECTING WORDS

A *preposition* takes a noun or pronoun as its object. It links the object to another word in the sentence and indicates the relation between them:

The displays *for* the exhibit sat *near* the door.

The key *to* it fell *behind* the chair.

He went *with* her.

A *conjunction* joins:

words: pen *and* pencil, fish *and* chips, tea *and* sympathy, right *and* wrong
phrases: in the warehouse *or* in the garage
clauses: We laughed *because* we were nervous. The men barbecued hamburgers, *and* the women made salads.

An *interjection* conveys emotion rather than thought. Though it is called a part of speech, it has no relation to the other words in a sentence. When used alone, it behaves almost like a sentence. For that reason interjections are a concern only in terms of punctuation:

Ouch!
Oh, what a chance!
Well, what now?

Complete Work Project 1

WORK PROJECT 1

Identifying Parts of Speech

A.   Write the name of the part of speech above each word in the following sentences. Do not label *a, an,* and *the.* They are always adjectives.

Noun	Verb	Adjective	Conjunction
Pronoun	Adverb	Preposition	Interjection

Ex: The   **new**   **watchman**   **checks**   **those**   **passes**   **carefully.**

(ADJ. N V ADJ. N ADV.)

1.   A financial report left this office yesterday.

2.   A red and yellow monogram embellishes the stationery.

3.   Mr. Goodson inquired casually about the expense.

4.   Miss Beals is the secretary to the manager.

5.   He sent the annual report to ten offices.

6.   Fenton or Johnson solved the difficulty very quickly.

7.   Some clients waited in the reception room for hours.

8.   The buzzer sounded loudly and clearly in the front office.

9.   Oh, she parked the car very carelessly and dented both fenders.

10.   She and the buyer decided against the new line of dresses.

B.   Supply a word for each part of speech left blank. If the word you supply fits the context of the sentence and makes sense, you have supplied the correct part of speech and proved your native grasp of grammar.

1.   A .... clerk .... us the address.
          (adj.)   *(verb)*

2.   Mr. Daws spoke .... about the loss .... his money.
                (adverb)   *(prep.)*

3.   .... walked .... the park during the .... period.
    (noun)   *(prep.)*   *(adj.)*

4. Brown .... black .... have been discounted 10 per cent for
              (conj.)   (noun)

    this ....
          (noun)

5. .... , what a day!
    (interj.)

C. Identify the part of speech of each word in italics.

1. *She* spoke to me *yesterday.*

2. Mr. Ringer *and* Miss Leslie have left.

3. The group was *silent.*

4. Miss Booth types *neatly.*

5. An *unusually* large man *approached* the desk.

6. *Well,* there you are!

7. The telephone rang intermittently *for* an hour.

8. I told *him* about it.

6

3 IDENTIFYING SUBJECTS AND VERBS

We communicate our thoughts to each other by naming what we want to talk about and then asserting something about what we have named. One way to simplify English is to start with the most fundamental fact about it: a sentence must contain a *subject* (the person or thing being talked about) and a *predicate* (what is said about the subject). With the subject and verb acting as a framework, we can then develop or refine a thought by adding words or word groups either to the subject or the predicate.

The subject of a sentence is easily located by asking the question *Who or what is being named for discussion?*

> Ex: Philip attended the meeting.
> (Who or what is being named for discussion? *Philip.*)

> Ex: The telephone is convenient.
> (Who or what is being named for discussion? *Telephone.*)

> Ex: The foreman has a problem.
> (Who or what is being named for discussion? *Foreman.*)

The predicate states something about the subject. The chief asserting word is the verb, which can indicate action, possession, or state of being. To locate the verb, ask the question *What is asserted about the subject?*

> Ex: The new clerk filed the correspondence.
> (What is asserted about the subject *clerk?* The clerk did what? *Filed the correspondence. Filed* is the verb, indicating action.)

> Ex: A committee had the report yesterday.
> (What is asserted about the subject *committee?* The committee had what? *Had the report yesterday. Had* is the verb, indicating possession.)

> Ex: Joan is friendly.
> (What is asserted about the subject *Joan?* Joan is what? *Is friendly. Is* indicates state of being.)

Verb Phrases

In order to complete its function, a verb often depends upon helping verbs such as *have, can, may, will, could, should, must, be,* and *do.* A verb and one or more helping words is called a *verb phrase.*

7

The verb as a single word: He *walks* to work.
He *walked* to work.

The verb as a phrase: He *is walking.*
He *has walked.*
He *can walk.*
He *should be walking.*
He *might have been walking.*
He *must have walked.*

Helping verbs work within the phrase to point out the time of an action or various shades of meaning:

Time: He *will walk.*   (future action)
He *is walking.*   (action going on at present)
He *has been walking.* (action begun in the past but continuing into the present)

Shade of meaning: He *can walk.*   (ability)
He *does walk.*   (emphasis)
He *might walk.*   (shade of doubt)
He *could walk.*   (possibility)
He *may walk.*   (permission or probability)
He *should walk.*   (duty or obligation)

Time and shade of meaning: He *might have been walking.*
He *should have walked.*
He *may be walking.*

Complete Work Project 2

WORK PROJECT 2

Identifying Subjects and Verbs

In each of the following sentences draw one line under the subject and two lines under the verb or verb phrases.

Ex: The new method has required less time.

Bill Alder received an expensive satchel.

1. Some unusual models have been introduced lately.

2. Mr. Cody revised his first estimate.

3. The missing papers were lying there.

4. Several mild complaints demanded his attention.

5. They should have routed the materials differently.

6. The interest is overdue.

7. My wife has her own car.

8. A checker should be catching the defective parts.

9. Mr. Wiley supervises the first operation.

10. September will have two holidays.

11. The old machine had performed poorly.

12. His appointment had been canceled.

13. The ink stained her dress.

14. Who is collecting our applications?

15. Miss Burns clutched her handbag nervously.

16. The two auditors were working independently.

17. A speech course might help you.

18. Someone should have typed that memorandum.

19. The custodian was late.

20. The company owns the patent rights.

21. Miss Burton has been improving her penmanship.

22. The identification labels have been altered.

23. Three members might withdraw their support.

24. Who should be monitoring this call?

25. The decision must be made quickly.

26. Mr. Daws will countersign your check.

27. Hughes Construction Company does accept its employees' suggestions.

28. Marvin can estimate the damage.

29. The experience was valuable.

30. Eleanor had the missing letter.

4 | THE BASIC SENTENCE PATTERNS

Though words and expressions go in and out of fashion, the structure of our language endures. This structure is determined by word order, the characteristic manner in which words are combined to express a thought, especially subjects and predicates. If a so-called thinking machine were oriented to analyze English sentences, it would produce some amazing statistics within a short time. No matter whether we fed it the Sunday comics, a *Reader's Digest,* the *Wall Street Journal,* or a literary classic, the results would be the same. The great bulk of sentences would be sorted into three main categories, and the balance of them would fall under the heading of variations.

Learning to recognize these three basic sentences patterns and then to use them consciously is an important step toward sentence mastery.

Pattern One

SUBJECT	VERB
The people	voted.
Mr. Smithers	retired.
I	left.
He	was speaking.
A correction	has been made.

Pattern Two

SUBJECT	VERB	OBJECT
Martha	borrowed	a mirror.
The auditor	will examine	the books.
Salesmen	have canvassed	the area.
The printer	supplies	the paper.

Note. The second pattern is merely an extension of the first. The action set in motion by a subject is often carried over to an object or receiver of the action. If a sentence contains the second pattern, then you can ask *whom?* or *what?* after the verb and expect an answer:

S	V		O
Mr. Austin	respected	(whom?)	Arnold.
They	like	(what?)	the challenge.

Pattern Three

SUBJECT	LINKING VERB	COMPLEMENT NOUN
Marsden	is	the director.
The truck	was	a Chevrolet.
Consultants	are	experts.
The inspector	has been	Mr. Roberts.

SUBJECT	LINKING VERB	COMPLEMENT PRONOUN
The applicant	is	he.
It	was	I.
The brothers	were	they.

SUBJECT	LINKING VERB	COMPLEMENT ADJECTIVE
The conference	was	successful.
She	is	late.
The mechanism	might have been	defective.

Note. A linking verb is simply a verb that indicates state of being. In the examples above the linking verb does not carry over action from the subject to an object. It does, however, link the subject with the complement, a word which helps the linking verb to complete its assertion about the subject. Think of a linking verb as an equals sign; it shows that the subject and the complement are balanced with each other:

> Harold   is   a lawyer.
>   (Harold = a lawyer)
>
> Harold   is   he.
>   (Harold = he)
>
> Harold   is   personable.
>   (Harold = personable)

The chief linking verbs come from the family of verbs called *to be: am, are, is, was, were,* and verb phrases ending in *be, being,* and *been* (*could be, have been, are being,* etc.).

Since the pronoun equals the subject, the complement pronoun is always in the subject case (*Harold is he, He is Harold*). *Harold is him* would be incorrect because *him* is not equal to the subject: ~~*Him*~~ *is Harold.*

Review

In the work projects you will be asked to complete, the sentences will be short ones at first. As we study the parts of speech and word groups, however, they will become increasingly longer and more varied. Do not think that sentence patterns occur only in brief constructions. You will see in the examples below that the sentence pattern has little or nothing to do with the length of a sophisticated sentence:

>   s   v
> The quaint little *town*, located along the Mexican border, *has disappeared* from the tourist guidebooks.
>
> s   v   o
> *Mr. Hall*, sensing the current business trend, *bought stock* in the newly formed corporation.
>
>   s   LV   CA
> My *partner*, a former supply officer, *is* very *competent* in handling freight.

VARIATIONS OF THE BASIC SENTENCE PATTERNS

As a native speaker of English, you probably never make a mistake in forming sentences which utilize variations of the basic sentence patterns. To gain a conscious mastery of structure, however, you need an awareness of what happens when we use "there" sentences, give commands or make requests, and ask questions.

"There" sentences

Occasionally *am, are, is, was, were,* etc. are used in first-pattern sentences. We can avoid confusing them with linking verbs if we remember that linking verbs *require* complements.

V	S		S	LV	CN
There	is	an obstacle.	The money	is	an obstacle.
There	could be	a mistake.	The veto	could be	a mistake.
There	has been	an advantage.	The delay	has been	an advantage.

In these sentences the word *there* takes the place of the shifted subject—which our sense of word order requires to begin a statement.

Commands and Requests

Since commands and requests are made directly to someone else, the subject *you* is left out of the sentence. The word *please* turns a command into a request. For the sake of simplicity, consider *please* as a helping verb.

S	LV	CA	S	V	S	V	O
(You)	Be	quiet.	(You)	Go.	(You)	Please sign	it.

Questions

With the proper voice inflection, nearly any statement can be converted into a question (The light is satisfactory?). More commonly we ask questions by a slight change in the basic pattern (Is the light satisfactory?). Frequently a question requires a special word at the beginning which may or may not be a part of the basic pattern. Study the illustrations below. The easiest way to identify the pattern in a question is to apply the familiar questions. *Who or what is being named for discussion?* and *What is asserted about the subject?*

	S	V or LV	O or C
Has the mail arrived?	Mail	has arrived	
Do you have the time?	you	do have	time
Were you comfortable?	you	were	comfortable
When did the lease expire?	lease	did expire	
Which hat did she buy?	she	did buy	hat
Where have you stayed?	you	have stayed	
Whose remark was that?	that	was	remark

OTHER LINKING VERBS

There are other verbs besides *to be* which can express state of being and thus connect subjects and complements. Many of them pertain to sensory perceptions:

to smell:	The ditto fluid *smells* good.
to feel:	This material *feels* rough.
to sound:	She *sounded* angry.
to look:	The paint *looks* wet.
to taste:	Her lemon pie *tastes* sour.
to remain:	You *have remained* silent.
to appear:	He *appeared* nervous.

Some of these same verbs can also be used to express action in a second-pattern sentence:

S   V   O
The bus driver sounded his horn.

S   V   O
I smelled the coffee.

S   V   O
Have you tasted the dessert?

To determine whether or not a verb is a linking verb, substitute for it the equivalent form of *to be*. If the meaning of the sentence remains basically the same, the verb is linking. If the meaning is changed so that it becomes absurd, then the verb under consideration expresses action and fits a S-V-O pattern:

S   LV   CA
(is)
The prospect looks bright.

S   LV   CA
(was)
The coffee smelled good.

S   V   O
(~~was~~)
She smelled the coffee.

S   V   O
(~~was~~)
The customer felt the fur.

Complete Work Projects 3 and 4

WORK PROJECT 3

Identifying the Basic Sentence Patterns

A. Write the basic patterns above the appropriate words in the following list of sentences. Note the abbreviations used in the guides.

```
         S         LV        CN
Ex:  Roger  Taylor  was  an  investor.
```

```
     S    LV    CA
He   was   foolhardy.
```

```
     S      V
He   speculated.
```

```
     S    V          O
He   lost   his   money.
```

```
         S      LV    CP
The   victim   was   he.
```

1. The   rent   is   due.

2. The   contractor   violated   our   agreement.

3. The   stock   market   gained.

4. Miss   Wilson   locked   the   door.

5. She   is   the   best   stenographer.

6. They   overlooked   a   bargain.

7. Two   agencies   have   been   created.

8. The   chart   is   helpful.

9. I   predict   a   change.

10. The   weather   has   changed.

11. Their   attitude   is   optimistic.

12. Who   wanted   coffee?

13. The   local   representative   is   Henry   Hartley.

14. The   winners   were   they.

15. Your brother is the mayor.

16. The local demand has dwindled.

17. The wholesale price is exhorbitant.

18. Four college graduates applied.

19. Numerous recommendations will be considered.

20. Civic responsibility is an important consideration.

B. Write the basic sentence patterns above the appropriate words in the following list of sentences. Note the abbreviations used in the guides. Some sentences will contain variations.

Ex:
     S   LV   CA   V   S
    That man was afraid.   There are two objections.

    (v)   S   V   O   (v)   S   (v)   V
    Did you see a taxi?   Where has he been hiding?

    (S) LV CA
    (You) Be still.

1. There is one answer.

2. Are they going?

3. When is the meeting?

4. Mary is often contrary.

5. Which typewriter did you use?

6. Charley was the culprit.

7. Why has the boss been grouchy?

8. Stay here.

9. Please stay here.

10. Is it cold?

11. Be careful.

12. There are four main suggestions.

13. Please hurry.

14. Which group did you approve?

15. Is Malcolm the owner?

16

16. Has the lunch buzzer sounded?

17. The odor is objectionable.

18. Stay.

19. Are the machines operating?

20. Do they have an account?

21. The line was busy.

22. Are the stencils ready?

23. Only four passengers disembarked.

24. There has been no improvement.

25. Three representatives are attending the conference.

26. Who heard his speech?

27. Does this drawer contain stationery?

28. Whom should we support?

29. When did he leave?

30. Where is the cafeteria?

WORK PROJECT 4

Identifying Other Linking Verbs

A. Underline the linking verbs in the following sentences and prove your answers by writing in above them the equivalent forms of *to be* that can be substituted for them without destroying the meaning. Some sentences will not contain linking verbs.

                  (were)   (will be)

Ex: The reports <u>appeared</u> brief.   I <u>will remain</u> patient.

                 (had been)   (was)

The dictation <u>had seemed</u> long.   He sounded the horn.

1. The young accountant looks uncertain.

2. The curious bear tasted the salad.

3. Her comment sounds typical.

4. He looked serious.

5. The delegates have remained calm.

6. The evening sky appeared stormy.

7. A courageous teller sounded the alarm.

8. Her skill seems adequate.

9. My leg had felt numb.

10. Many older employees will remain sympathetic.

B. If you have worked these first ten sentences correctly, you should have little trouble deciding on the linking verbs in the following ten sentences.

1. James Perry became our first member.

2. The registration list grew long.

3. The treasurer approved the disbursement.

4. Our cafeteria will stay open.

5. One custodian kept the keys.

6. One man kept silent.

7. The nights turned cold.

8. He fell silent.

9. My hunch proved right.

10. The machine went wild.

B.   As a means of demonstrating your grasp of the material presented to date, you are asked to compose short sentences of your own in the spaces provided below. When you are in doubt, feel free to turn back to the explanatory material for illustrations. If you find a S-V-O pattern illustrated with "John designs containers," then you might write "Margaret supplies the blanks."

PATTERN ONE: S   V

1. ....

2. ....

PATTERN TWO: S   V   O

1. ....

2. ....

PATTERN THREE: S   LV   CN

1. ....

2. ....

                                      S   LV   CP

1. ....

2. ....

                                      S   LV   CA

1. ....

2. ....

A REQUEST OR COMMAND (any pattern):

....

A QUESTION (any pattern):

....

A "THERE" SENTENCE (S-V):

....

A SENTENCE CONTAINING THE LINKING VERB *looks* (S-LV-CA):

....

20

5   NOUNS

Studying the parts of speech serves two objectives: it helps to deepen our grasp of sentence structure and it enables us to eliminate common errors in our writing and speaking.

It is logical to begin a study of the parts of speech with nouns because they are the most numerous words in our language. They are also the most basic. Children usually begin their vocabularies by identifying important or fascinating "things" in their environment: *mama, papa, toy, cat, dog.* Naming a thing gives us a degree of power over it because we are then able to sort it out readily from the multitude of other things that claim our attention. You now have thousands of "namers" at your command and absorb new ones almost automatically. Traditionally nouns are identified according to the following categories:

PERSON	ANIMAL	THING	PLACE	GROUP	QUALITY OR IDEA
girl	bear	desk	country	pair	pride
model	tadpole	cup	city	trio	capitalism
father	eagle	tray	lake	audience	reliability
salesman	snake	warehouse	peninsula	team	democracy

Nouns are distinguished as *common* or *proper*. A common noun names one member of a general class; a proper noun gives a particular name to one member of a general class:

COMMON:	salesman	horse	company	river	team	pride
PROPER:	Mr. Reed	Whirlaway	Smith & Son	Red River	the Giants	

Note. Especially in poetry, some qualities or ideas are personified and therefore capitalized: "And Justice wept at her own cruel measure."

How Nouns Can Contribute to Your Writing Proficiency

The difference between acceptable writing and indifferent writing is often a small one if we measure it by the number of mistakes made. In handling nouns, for example, a poor writer may err in only two out of a hundred per page. Such is the nature of a native grasp of English, however, that even a relatively uneducated person can distinguish correct writing from incorrect on a small amount of evidence—even though he himself cannot explain what is wrong or how to correct it! The explanation is simple: most if not all the printed matter we read daily follows accepted conventions, and the writer who disregards them puts an extra burden on the reader to decipher the writer's intention.

For most people, nouns become a problem because it is easy to confuse a plural noun (two attorneys) with a possessive noun (the attorney's office). Even more confusion arises when they are confronted with a need for a plural possessive noun (the two attorneys' opinions). A few people avoid the problem by putting an apostrophe after *any* noun ending in *s*. (In desperation, some people even add the apostrophe to verbs ending in *s*: He pays' the bill.) Students have been known to beg the question by placing an apostrophe above the *s* in a possessive noun in the hope that the teacher will accept the apostrophe as being either before the *s* or after it, depending on which position is correct:

<u>The mans̓ work has been completed.</u>

Learning to use plurals and possessives correctly is quite simple. Reviewing the ways of forming English plurals will give you a good foundation for studying possessives, since the two areas are so closely related. Once you have absorbed the principles presented in this section, your own writing should show perceptible improvement almost overnight.

FORMING THE PLURALS OF NOUNS

The experts tell us that English is an eclectic language; that is, it readily borrows words from other languages. This borrowing began many centuries ago and continues today. Complications in spelling plurals (and other words) are explained by the fact that the process of borrowing has gone on in a spontaneous, haphazard fashion. What we think of as being the chaos in English spelling turns out to be a reflection of the various other languages from which English has refreshed itself. One word might have been adopted with its original pronunciation and spelling. Another might have retained its original pronunciation but changed to a more typical English spelling. Still others might have lost both the original pronunciation and spelling.

Regardless of their origin, most English nouns conform to a standard pattern: they become plural by adding *s* or *es*. Only a few hundred nouns are irregular. Fortunately, most of these are everyday words you seldom have to think about. With the exception of the *y* ending, the categories of noun plurals listed below are intended as convenient groupings, not as spelling rules. The lists are not exhaustive, but they do contain the most troublesome words. Read through them carefully. If you come across one of your own "thorns," underline it and associate it in your mind with other words in the same grouping.

1.   The great bulk of English nouns become plural merely by the addition of *s*:

office, offices	change, changes	manager, managers	brain, brains
typist, typists	fee, fees	executive, executives	desk, desks
John Smith, the Smiths		specimen, specimens	

2.   Nouns that end in *s, x, z, ch,* or *sh* form the plural by adding *es*. Since these words already end in an *s* sound, the voice requires the addition of the vowel sound to glide smoothly from one *s* sound to the other:

branch, branches	tax, taxes	brush, brushes	Tom Jones
business, businesses	buzz, buzzes	crunch, crunches	the Joneses

3.   Nouns ending in *y* preceded by a consonant form their plural by changing *y* to *i* and adding *es*. Nouns ending in *y* preceded by a vowel merely add *s*:

company, companies	alloy, alloys
specialty, specialties	attorney, attorneys
reply, replies	delay, delays

Note. It is not acceptable to change the spelling of a proper name. Beware of adding an *ies* ending to a proper name ending in *y*:

John Fry, the Frys
Not
the Fries (another name, pronounced freeze)

4. The majority of nouns ending in *o* merely add *s*; a few add *es*. The simplest way to gain control over these words is to study the exceptions carefully; all other *o* words can then be assumed to fit the rule.

Exceptions:	Words regularly adding *s*:
buffaloes	cameos
cargoes (cargos)	crescendos
desperadoes	dynamos
echoes	embryos
embargoes	mementos
heroes	pianos
innuendoes	portfolios
manifestoes	radios
mottoes	solos
mosquitoes	sopranos
potatoes	studios
Negroes	tobaccos
noes	trios
tomatoes	zeros
tornadoes	
torpedoes	
vetoes	
volcanoes	

5. Approximately half the commonly used words ending in *f* or *fe* add *s*; the other half change the *f* to *v* and add *s* or *es*:

Words adding *s*:	Words changing f to v:
belief, beliefs	calf, calves
brief, briefs	half, halves
bailiff, bailiffs	knife, knives
chief, chiefs	leaf, leaves
chef, chefs	loaf, loaves
cliff, cliffs	life, lives
dwarf, dwarfs	scarf, scarves (first choice)
handkerchief, handkerchiefs	shelf, shelves
plaintiff, plaintiffs	thief, thieves
proof, proofs	wharf, wharves (first choice)
roof, roofs	
safe, safes	
hoof, hoofs (first choice)	

6. Some extremely common nouns form their plurals by a change in the spelling:

foot, feet	mouse, mice	tooth, teeth
man, men	goose, geese	woman, women

7. Two nouns add *en*:   child, children   ox, oxen

8.   A few nouns exist only in the plural form:

auspices	credentials	premises	riches
assets	goods	proceeds	scissors
cattle	headquarters	trousers	thanks

Note.   As subjects, these nouns require a plural verb:

The scissors are on the table.
The premises have been searched thoroughly.

9.   Some nouns are plural in form but are used with a singular meaning:

athletics	ethics	mathematics	measles	news	politics
electronics	economics	molasses	mumps	physics

Note.   As subjects, these nouns require a singular verb:

Athletics has always been my best subject.
Politics often affects business.

10.   Some nouns have the same form for both the singular and plural:

corps, deer, Chinese, fish, gross, salmon, sheep, species, swine, trout, series

Note.   It is possible to use *fishes* to denote more than one species of fish. This use is relatively uncommon.

New Zealand's rivers are filled with dozens of *fishes*.

11.   Compound words add *s* to the principal word or change the spelling of the principal word:

sister-in-law, sisters-in-law	court-martial, courts-martial
editor-in-chief, editors-in-chief	lieutenant commander,
passer-by, passers-by	lieutenant commanders
workman, workmen	step-son, step-sons
Frenchman, Frenchmen	secretary of state,
German, Germans	secretaries of state

12.   Compound words used to indicate measurement or quantity add *s* to ful:

cupfuls, barrelfuls, mouthfuls, handfuls, teaspoonfuls, armfuls

13.   Infrequently a compound word requires a plural in both parts:

manservant, menservants   Knight Templar, Knights Templars

14.   An appreciable number of foreign nouns (borrowings) retain their foreign plural forms. A few of these have also acquired acceptable English forms as second choice. Study the pattern of change in the following groups:

is to *es:*	analysis, analyses	parenthesis, parentheses
	axis, axes	synopsis, synopses
	basis, bases	synthesis, syntheses
	crisis, crises	thesis, theses
	hypothesis, hypotheses	
um to *a:*	addendum, addenda	medium, media (mediums)
	bacterium, bacteria	memorandum, memoranda (memorandums)
	curriculum, curricula (curriculums)	referendum, referenda (referendums)
	datum, data	stratum, strata

us to *i:*	alumnus, alumni
	fungus, fungi
	stimulus, stimuli
on to *a:*	criterion, criteria (criterions)
	phenomenon, phenomena
x to *ces:*	appendix, appendices (appendixes)
	index, indices (indexes)
a to *ae:*	alumna, alumnae
	larva, larvae
	vertebra, vertebrae

15. Modern usage tends to avoid pluralized titles of address like the following:

Mr., Messrs. (Messieurs):	We have communicated with the Messrs. Winston and Brown.
Mrs., Mmes. (Mesdames):	The Mmes. Harry Worthington and Charley Brown visited relatives in Springdale over the weekend.
Miss, Misses:	This correspondence was initiated by the Misses Hardy.
	Misses Theresa and Marsha Goodman
	126 Alabama Avenue
	Marshall, Indiana
Preferred:	We have communicated with Mr. Winston and Mr. Brown.
	Mrs. Harry Worthington and Mrs. Charley Brown visited relatives in Springdale over the weekend.
	Miss Theresa and Miss Marsha Goodman
	126 Alabama Avenue
	Marshall, Indiana

Complete Work Project 5

FORMING AND USING POSSESSIVE NOUNS

Believe it or not, no native speaker of English makes a mistake in forming possessive nouns in routine conversation. When our ears pick up a noun ending in a sibilant or hiss sound (as in the letter *s*) followed by another noun, we recognize immediately that ownership or possession is being denoted:

Harold's girlfriend borrowed her brother's car.

Writing requires an additional sign—the apostrophe—to denote whether the possession is singular or plural in nature:

Harold's girlfriend borrowed her brother's car.   (one brother)
Harold's girlfriend borrowed her brothers' car.   (two brothers)

Since most plural nouns end in *s*, the problem in forming possessive nouns is to determine where to place the apostrophe—before the *s* or after it. The two following principles should prevent confusion:

Determine from the context whether a word is singular or plural. Does it end in *s?* If not, add *'s.*

- Nouns not already ending in *s* add *'s* to form the possessive.

    Determine from the context whether a word is singular or plural. Does it end in *s?* If so, merely add an apostrophe.

- Nouns already ending in *s* merely add an apostrophe to form the possessive.

NOUN IN CONTEXT	SINGULAR?	PLURAL?	END IN s?	POSSESSIVE
one mans family	X(one man)		no	man's
two mens families		X(two men)	no	men's
a boys bicycle	X(a boy)		no	boy's
three boys bicycles		X(three boys)	yes	boys'
Mr. Jones objection	X(Mr. Jones)		yes	Mr. Jones'
the Smiths car		X(the Smiths)	yes	Smiths'
the Joneses objection		X(the Joneses)	yes	Joneses'
my son-in-laws boy	X(son-in-law)		no	son-in-law's
my sons-in-laws boys		X(sons-in-law)	no	sons-in-law's

Note. If you prefer to say *Mr. Jones(uz) objection* because it sounds less awkward, then form the possessive like this: *Mr. Jones's* objection. The *'s* is used here to indicate the added *s* sound. This form can be used only with singular nouns: *Mr. Fass's office, Miss Durgess's telephone.*

Special Problems in Using Possessives

1. If two or more nouns are joined by *and,* use the apostrophe with the last noun to indicate *joint* possession:

    We agreed to meet at Hal, Bill, and Arnold's apartment.
    Jones and Culler's store is having a linen sale.

If two or more nouns are joined by *and,* use the apostrophe with each noun to indicate *separate* possession:

    Mr. Sloan approved of Mildred's and Sonia's clothes.
    The clerks' and secretaries' paychecks were ready for distribution.

2.   The possessive case is often used with nouns naming inanimate objects to express time or distance:

a stone's throw	ten minutes' time
a day's drive	a week's vacation
a two miles' journey	a three months' leave

With these exceptions, most writers avoid using inanimate objects as possessives:

Awkward:	the table's style
	the roses' fragrance
Preferred:	the style of the table
	the fragrance of the roses

3. Add *'s* to the abbreviations in proper names like these:

    John Howard, Jr.'s credit card
    Milton Thomas, Sr.'s retirement

4.   A possessive word may not always be followed by the object being owned, but the noun it limits should be found within the sentence:

That book is Sandra's.

The last appointment was Mr. Hammer's.

5.   In general, rewrite any possessive constructions involving an awkward use of the apostrophe:

John, my barber's, explanation. . . .
Preferred: The explanation given by John, my barber. . . .

Distinguishing between Plural Nouns and Possessives

To distinguish between a plural and a possessive word, apply this simple test. If the possessive word is used correctly, the possession can also be stated in an *of* phrase:

John left on a two weeks' vacation.
(a vacation *of two weeks*) ˙

John will be gone for two weeks.
(nothing is stated as being *of two weeks*)

Complete Work Project 6

THE FUNCTIONS OF NOUNS

Consider these four sentences:

The old *home* withstood the storm.

The children went *home*.

Home the ball to me.

Her doctor prescribed a *home* remedy.

Previously a noun was defined as a word that named a person, place, thing, etc. This definition cannot be applied automatically, however, as the sentences above illustrate. Only the *home* in the first sentence is used as a noun; it is the only *home* used in a noun position:

S   V   O
The old *home* withstood the storm.

S   V   ADV.
The children went *home*.

(S)   V   O
(You)   *Home* the ball to me.

S   V   ADJ.   O
Her doctor prescribed a *home* remedy.

It is possible, therefore, to base a more meaningful set of definitions of the parts of speech on the principle of word order—the characteristic position a particular word occupies in relation to other words in the same sentence. Nouns are easily identified in a sentence on the basis of the position they occupy. They function as subjects, objects of the verb, complement nouns, objects of a preposition, or appositives:

Subject

s	v		s	v	s	LV CP

The *applause* terminated.   *Mr. Hanson* spoke quietly.   The *fault* is mine.

- A subject normally comes before the verb or linking verb.

Object

s	v	o	s	v	o	s	v o

You bought the *store*.   He hid the *coin*.   They sold *parts*.

- The object comes after the verb in the S-V-O pattern.

Complement Noun

s	LV	CN	s	LV	CN

Alfred is a *musician*.   Mr. Putnam has been the *representative*.

- The complement noun comes after a linking verb.

Object of a Preposition

The dues for the *club* have been paid by *check*.

Note.   A prepositional phrase is a group of words beginning with a preposition and ending with an object. Such a phrase becomes a single unit of logic. For example, in the sentence *The man behind the counter laughed at our mistake,* if we take out the sentence pattern *man laughed,* we have left two logical thought units, *behind the counter* and *at our mistake. Behind the counter* modifies *man* and *at our mistake* modifies *laughed.* It is clear, then, that a prepositional phrase generally occurs after the word it modifies:

The man *behind the counter* laughed *at our mistake.*

Later we will discuss prepositions and prepositional phrases more fully, but at present it is important to be able to identify them in order to understand the role nouns play in sentence structure.

Appositive

My cousin, a *singer*, lives in Hollywood.   I like curry, an Indian *dish*.

Note.   An appositive is a word or word group that renames or reidentifies the noun it follows.

THE VERBAL NOUN

Everything that we have said about nouns in general also applies to a special kind of naming word called the verbal noun. As the term implies, this is a noun that is derived from a verb but is used as a noun. It is a naming word rather than an asserting word and functions as a subject, an object, a complement noun, an object of a preposition, or an appositive:

s	v

Singing as a verb: We *have been singing* for an hour.

Singing as a noun:
      S   LV CA
      Singing is fun.

      S V   O
      I like your *singing*.

        S   LV   CN
      His talent is his singing.

       S   V   O   OP
      He earned money by *singing*.

        S   APPOS.   V   O
      My avocation, *singing*, suits me.

A proper name or another noun used with a verbal noun should take the possessive form:

We listened to John's singing.

Miss Gordon's complaining annoyed us.

I stopped the man's arguing.

Complete Work Projects 7 and 8

WORK PROJECT 5

Forming the Plurals of Nouns

A. Opposite each word in the following list write its plural form. If a word already exists in the plural form, or if a word is never used in the plural form or meaning, leave the space blank. If a word seems difficult or if it is unfamiliar, try to recall another word like it. For instance, if you see that *synthesis* is like *analysis*, then the plural is likely to be *syntheses*, corresponding to *analyses*. If you cannot remember any similar words, look back at the explanatory material until you find the word itself or the category of words which it fits. To be sure, consult a dictionary.

1.	ledger	26.	loaf ....
2.	majority	27.	headquarters ....
3.	chintz	28.	politics ....
4.	quantity	29.	court-martial ....
5.	Clary	30.	alumnus ....
6.	Appley	31.	appendix ....
7.	touch	32.	roof ....
8.	wax	33.	memento ....
9.	housewife	34.	alumna ....
10.	specimen	35.	ethics ....
11.	species	36.	dwarf ....
12.	stimulus	37.	Japanese ....
13.	son-in-law	38.	datum ....
14.	echo	39.	synopsis ....
15.	innuendo	40.	rinse ....
16.	studio	41.	foundry ....
17.	premises	42.	mosquito ....
18.	vice-president	43.	journey ....
19.	syllabus	44.	Jones ....
20.	gross	45.	truth ....
21.	sheep	46.	major-general ....
22.	crisis	47.	resident ....
23.	phenomenon	48.	manservant ....
24.	spoonful	49.	gladiolus ....
25.	repairman	50.	mumps ....

B.   In the blanks at the right, fill in the correct plural forms of the words given in parentheses. Use foreign plurals for foreign words.

1. Our (laboratory) have made extensive (analysis) of these materials.

....

....

2. The (serviceman) responded with (crescendo) of laughter.

....

....

3. Two (lieutenant colonel) named their (beneficiary).

....

....

4. The three (daughter-in-law) were all (alumna) of an Eastern finishing school.

....

....

5. The (Merry) bought (cameo) instead of precious stones.

....

....

6. (Appendix) were included in both (thesis).

....

....

7. Two major (studio) filmed the (phenomenon).

....

....

8. The (motto) were suggested by two of our own (tradesman).

....

....

9. What are your (criterion) for choosing mild (tobacco)?

....

....

10. The (Madison) own a chain of (haberdashery).

....

....

C.   There is an incorrect plural form in each of the following sentences. Underline it and write in the correct form in the blank at the right.

1. His hypothesises about potatoes were correct.   ....

2. The Eskimos weathered both crisis.   ....

3. Our ten sheep are healthy specimen.   ....

4. The new supplies were divided between both shelfs.   ....

5. The necessary ratios were noted on several recent memorandas.   ....

6. Few attornies checked the list of casualties.   ....

7. The branches of the company have ordered a hundred grosses of letterhead paper.   ....

8. Two tablespoonsful of castor oil cured the little desperadoes.   ....

9. The tornadoes left the rooves covered with leaves.   ....

10. The embargoes were lifted on all radioes.   ....

D.   The titles of address used in the following items are too formal and stilted to suit the current taste. Change them to more acceptable forms in the spaces provided.

Ex: The invitations were designed by the Mmes. Funk and Lord.

....by Mrs. Funk and Mrs. Lord...

1.   We had a long conversation with the Misses Janet and Margaret Castle about their father's will.

    ....

2.   The Mmes. John Dowe and Henry Green spent last weekend at the home of Miss Susan West.

    ....

3.   A representative of our firm has already called on the Mmes. Henderson and West.

    ....

4.   Did you send the letters to the Misses Mayhew and Marks?

    ....

5.   Messrs. Robert and Franklin Pringle
    120 Main Street
    Springfield, Massachusetts

    ....

WORK PROJECT 6

Forming and Using Possessive Nouns

A.   Fill in the blank spaces with the appropriate forms. Look at the ending of a word as a singular or as a plural. Does it already end in s? If so, merely add the apostrophe. If not, add *'s*.

SINGULAR	SINGULAR POSSESSIVE	PLURAL	PLURAL POSSESSIVE
girl	girl's	girls	girls'
mother-in-law	....	....	....
Harold	....	....	....
woman	....	....	....
Johnson	....	....	....
attorney	....	....	....
baby	....	....	....
sheep	....	....	....
soprano	....	....	....
Jones	....	....	....

B.   Prove that the italicized words in the following sentences are correctly used as possessives by writing "of" phrases in the spaces provided below each sentence.

Ex: The paint was sent to the *Smiths'* home.

the home of the Smiths
....

1.   My two *weeks'* vacation was very restful.

....

2.   Who can solve *Henry's* problem?

....

3.   *Mr. Carruthers'* attitude was not sympathetic.

....

4.   We were interested in only two *senators'* speeches.

....

5.   No one doubted the *manager's* judgment.

....

C. Change the following *of* phrases into possessive nouns:

Ex: the books of the girl .... the girl's books ....

1. the account of the two women ....
2. the bill of the patient ....
3. the photograph of the Joneses ....
4. the report of Jack and Robert ....
5. the reports of Jack and Robert (separate ownership) ....

D. Each of the following sentences contains a possessive noun. If it is formed and used correctly, leave the space at the right blank. If the possessive is not called for or is incorrectly formed, make the correction in the space at the right.

Ex: The first applicant's record has been filed. ....
The conference lasted for three days'. .... days ....

The Brown's former home has been remodeled. .... Browns' ....

The table's color is quite pleasing. .... color of the table ....

1. Your brother's-in-law package was delivered. ....
2. There was an antique finish on the picture's frame. ....
3. Several workers were away for four days'. ....
4. There is room in it for a persons' valuables. ....
5. Barney Gould, Jr.'s proposal was accepted. ....
6. Did your groceries come from Todd's and Mason's store? ....
7. The children's floor is in the other wing. ....
8. He has the experience of eighteen years' behind him. ....
9. Mr. Jone's opinion was not the popular one. ....
10. They recorded the members' dues regularly. ....
11. That misplaced typewriter brush was Harry's. ....
12. Don Hartman has been added to the salesmens' division. ....
13. The vice-presidents' position has been newly created. ....
14. Miss Hawks caught her boss's mistake. ....
15. I have your telephone number but not your wife's. ....
16. The mens' interviews are scheduled for ten o'clock. ....
17. The belt's buckle was broken. ....
18. The annual stockholder's bulletin was eliminated from their envelopes. ....

36

19. John and Harry's daughters were both married last week. ....

20. You are faced with a long journey of two miles on foot. ....

21. Most people applauded the heroes' words before he had quite finished speaking. ....

22. The young reporter smarted over the editor-in-chief's deletions. ....

23. Please hand me the Murphys' order. ....

24. Mark Roberts wrote an amusing article for the company newspaper called "Mr. Robert's Headache."

25. Last months' trip won us many new agencies. ....

E. Compose a short sentence for each of the words in parentheses. Incorporate each word as a possessive noun.

Ex: (Tom)   We have returned Tom's calculations.

1. (women) ....
   ....

2. (Hersheys) ....
   ....

3. (Albert and Son) ....
   ....

4. (Ted and Mabel) (separate ownership) ....
   ....

5. (Ted and Mabel) (joint ownership) ....
   ....

WORK PROJECT 7

Identifying Nouns on the Basis of Word Order and Classifying Them According to Function

A. Underline each noun in the following sentence and identify its function.

Ex: A $\underset{\text{s}}{\underline{\text{messenger}}}$ delivered the $\underset{\text{o}}{\underline{\text{telegram}}}$ to the $\underset{\text{OP}}{\underline{\text{superintendent}}}$.

$\underset{\text{s}}{\underline{\text{Hillary}}}$, a former $\underset{\text{APPOS.}}{\underline{\text{athlete}}}$, disapproved of my $\underset{\text{OP}}{\underline{\text{smoking}}}$.

1. Miss Sparks, the supervisor, checks our typing closely.

2. The two receptionists were attractive girls with pleasant voices.

3. These invoices on my desk require immediate handling.

4. The customer returned with her husband before deciding.

5. Susan's approach is direct.

6. The broker guaranteed a satisfactory return for our investment.

7. Frank's joking eased the tension in the stockroom.

8. The switchboard operator, Carroll Davis, corrected my misdialing.

9. A metallurgical laboratory tested the tensile strength of this new alloy.

10. The testimony of Ralph Pierson, the chief witness, impressed the jury.

B. Construct a sentence for each of the words listed below. Incorporate each in such a manner that it functions as indicated.

Ex: (fairness) Mr. Dean commanded respect by his $\underset{\text{OP}}{\text{fairness}}$.

(neighbor) Mrs. Williams, my $\underset{\text{APPOS.}}{\text{neighbor}}$, asked for advice.

1. $\underset{\text{s}}{\text{management}}$ ....

2. $\underset{\text{APPOS.}}{\text{talking}}$ ....

3. drivers ....

4. driving ....

5. headquarters ....

C. Place apostrophes where they are required in the following passage.

Miss Johnsons typing is better than Miss Carsons filing, but both clerks could benefit from Mrs. Jones training in secretarial practice. An employees returning to school for additional preparation is well received in the front office.

WORK PROJECT 8

Correcting Copy

The following letter contains many errors in forming and using plurals and possessives. Place a check mark ($\sqrt{}$) after the number of each line that contains one or more errors.

NINE PINES
HYBRIDIZING GARDENS

Boring, Oregon

August 15, 19—

Dear Friends:

We hope you will like the new catalog which we are	1 ....
enclosing. In it you will find many new lilys, daffodils,	2 ....
and hardy perennials' which we are putting on the market for	3 ....
the first time. We have benefited from an unusually favorable	4 ....
growing season and have large stock of all items.	5 ....
As you know, lily breeding is one of our family specialtys.	6 ....
Estrelita, a large lily of pale pink, is my son's-in-laws best	7 ....
achievement to date. It is the cross of two specieses, auratum	8 ....
and speciosum. Green Dragon, a huge sulfur trumpet lily, is	9 ....
everybodys' favorite. This flower's fragrance is something to	10 ....
inhale! Three bulbs of this variety will produce armsful of	11 ....
cut flowers that will last in water for many days. Martha's	12 ....
Favorite is just that—a mouth-watering golden yellow tigrinum	13 ....
hybird whose daintiness stimulates every womans' desire to make	14 ....
an arrangement.	15 ....
My two son's daffodil breeding program has just begun to	16 ....
reap rewards in the last two years'. The King's Champion,	17 ....
Henry's first introduction, is a phenomena in size of bloom and	18 ....

purity of color. The perianth is five inch across; the trumpet   19 ....

is of noble proportions; and the entire flower is white as snow.   20 ....

Rogers first introduction is called Sweet Sixteen in honor of   21 ....

his first girlfriend. The blossoms are white with salmon-pink   22 ....

cups of exceptional refinement. I know you will be pleased   23 ....

with both Henry and Roger's introductions.   24 ....

    Of course, we continue to offer the best varieties of   25 ....

hardy perennials, including several exciting new dwarves.   26 ....

Our customers letters give glowing reports about the perfor-   27 ....

mance of our plants.   28 ....

    Our nursery fields and trial beds are located only a ten 29 ....

minutes drive from Boring. The daffodils are at their best in   30 ....

late May; the lilies, in early August. Plan to visit us this   31 ....

year. The Caries will be glad to welcome you.   32 ....

Cordially,

Malcolm Cary

Malcolm Cary

Enclosure

In the spaces provided below, first list the number of the line which contains error(s). Then supply the correction(s) in the other spaces.

Ex: ......2.....   ....lilies.....................   ....

    ....

    ....

    ....

    ....

    ....

    ....

    ....

6   PRONOUNS

Pronouns are extremely useful words that substitute for nouns. Without them our writing would be burdened with the necessity of continually identifying people, places, and things. Imagine your annoyance at having to commuicate with sentences like this one: *Mr. Allen said that Mr. Allen had taken Mr. Allen's wife with Mr. Allen when Mr. Allen first went to Australia.* How much more convenient it is to avoid the repetition of nouns: *Mr. Allen said that he had taken his wife with him when he first went to Australia.*

How Pronouns Can Contribute to Your Writing Proficiency

Since pronouns are so central to our writing and so few in number, errors in using them are not casually overlooked. "*Him* and Ted left early for the ball game" would probably not cost you a friend or a job, but it and similar errors would disqualify you as a likely candidate for an executive position requiring letter writing. And even an accomplished dictator wants to have a stenographer who can catch and correct his occasional slips. The person who has to stop for a minute to decide on a correct pronoun (*who* or *whom?* *we* or *us?*) is not being businesslike: he is wasting time and cutting down his own efficiency.

Pronouns, unlike nouns, often change form in order to perform as subjects, objects, or complements. They also change form according to number, person, and gender. Further, there are the problems involved in determining the correct antecedent, in making the pronoun agree with its antecedent, and in choosing the correct form of *who/whom* and *whoever/ whomever.*

Mastering pronouns will be easy because what you have learned about nouns in the preceding section will transfer readily to pronouns, and the basic sentence patterns will prove to be an infallible guide in deciding on correct pronoun case. If you are an average person, you will discover at least one or two ways in which you have been misusing pronouns. Conscious effort will quickly eliminate these from your writing and—more gradually—from your speaking.

THE FUNCTIONS OF PRONOUNS

Pronouns follow the same word order as nouns and function in an identical manner:

           S   V   S   LV   CN   S   V
Subject: *He* spoke. *It* was a problem. *We* did not protest.

- A pronoun serving as a subject normally comes before the verb or linking verb.

S   V   O   S   V   O
Object of a verb: The company promoted *him*. John greeted *us*.

- A pronoun serving as an object comes after the verb in a S-V-O pattern.

S   LV CP S LV CP
Complement: The salesman was *he*. It was *I*.

- A complement pronoun comes after the linking verb.

OP   OP
Object of a preposition: Mr. Johns agrees with *her*. I left before *them*.

- A pronoun serving as the object of a preposition comes after the preposition.

Note.   A pronoun is not used as an appositive because it replaces a noun already used, whereas an appositive renames or reidentifies a person, place, or thing already cited.

THE CHARACTERISTICS OF PRONOUNS

A pronoun is controlled to a great extent by the noun it replaces, its *antecedent:*

> *Ethel* and her *mother* canceled *their* insurance policies.

> *Mr. Perkins* exchanged *his* Christmas ties for shirts.

A pronoun must always agree with its antecedent in *person, number,* and *gender:*

Person: *I* (the first person, the person speaking) asked *you* (the second person, the person spoken to) about *him* (the third person, the person being spoken about).

Number: *She* (singular) liked *them* (plural).

Gender: *She* (feminine) bought the sweater and mailed *it* (sexlessness) to *him* (masculine).

Unlike nouns, which remain unchanged, pronouns often take different forms to serve their different functions or *cases:*

> *He* (subject case) telephoned *us* (object case) about *his* (possessive case) difficulty.

> The decision was *mine* (possessive case).

These important characteristics are described in the following lists:

		SUBJECT CASE	OBJECT CASE	POSSESSIVE CASE
SINGULAR	1	I	me	my, mine
	2	you	you	your, yours
	3	she, he, it	her, him, it	his, her, hers, its
PLURAL	1	we	us	our, ours
	2	you	you	your, yours
	3	they	them	their, theirs
EITHER		who	whom	whose

Note 1.   *Who, whom,* and *whose* are the forms employed when the speaker cannot identify the person, number, or gender. They are especially useful in questions.

Note 2.   Normally possessive nouns occur before the thing being possessed (*Mr. Kurt's journal*) but can occur in the complement after a linking verb (The journal was *Mr. Kurt's*). Similarly, possessive pronouns occur in the same positions, but some of them change form when they are used in the complement (*My* journal disappeared. The missing journal is *mine*).

ERRORS IN CASE

Our acutely developed sense of what sounds right can normally be counted on to help us choose the correct case of a pronoun:

> *He* ordered a special magazine rack.
>
> *We* changed the furniture around.
>
> The delegates were *they*.
>
> The adjustment letter was returned to *me*.

Errors in choosing the correct case usually occur when there is a noun working with the pronoun in a compound subject or object or complement. Sometimes a qualifying word is used after the pronoun. In both instances our aural sense of correctness is disrupted:

> ~~Him~~ and John ordered a special magazine rack.
>
>   (A noun is used in the compound subject.)
>
> ~~Us~~ fellows changed the furniture around.
>
>   (*Fellows* is a qualifying word.)
>
> The delegates were Mr. Hawkins and ~~them~~.
>
>   (A noun is used in the compound complement.)
>
> The adjustment letter was returned to Miss Walker and ~~I~~.
>
>   (A noun is used in the compound object of a preposition.)

Errors like those above are easily avoided by ignoring the qualifying word or the noun used as the other subject or object. The correct case is then apparent:

> *Him* . . . ordered a special magazine rack? (*Him* cannot serve as a subject)
>
> *Us* . . . changed the furniture around? (*Us* cannot serve as a subject)
>
> The delegates were . . . *them?* (*Them* cannot serve as a complement pronoun)
>
> The adjustment letter was returned to . . . *I?* (*I* cannot serve as an object of a preposition)

The case of a pronoun used in a comparison is easily determined if you will remember that the pronoun is the subject of a sentence pattern which is understood or implied:

> Hazel Brown is as competent as *she*. (is competent)
>
> My brother speaks better French than *I*. (speak French)

Occasionally a pronoun used in a comparison is the object of a verb or a preposition in a pattern which is understood or implied:

The president conferred with him as well as *her*.
  (The president conferred with him . . . with her.)

Hogan liked her better than *me*.
  (Hogan liked her . . . liked me.)

Complete Work Project 9

-SELF WORDS

Thinking that *I* is an immodest word, many people fall into an awkward use of *myself* in order to avoid calling attention to themselves: Mr. Martin, Mr. Thomas, and *myself* attended the luncheon. This practice is ungrammatical and thus calls undue attention to itself.

There are two valid purposes for *-self* words, to show emphasis and to refer the action back to the subject:

Emphasis: The customers *themselves* caught the mistake.
             The owner *himself* approached us.

Reflexive action: I scolded *myself* for my behavior.
             The children chose the present by *themselves*.

The following words are not acceptable in standard English and should be avoided:

Mr. Clyde was muttering to ~~*hisself*~~.

The carpenters ~~*themself*~~ disapproved of the plans.

We ~~*ourself*~~ agreed with others.

They arranged for the banquet all by ~~*themselfs*~~.

Will they remind ~~*theirselves*~~ of the meeting?

WHO AND WHOM

Utilizing the basic sentence patterns can almost immediately clear up any uncertainty you may presently have with respect to *who* and *whom*, even in conversation.

Who is a subject case pronoun corresponding to *he* or *they*. In fact, one test for the correctness is to substitute *he* or *they* for *who*:

S	V	O		S	LV	CP
(He)					(he)	
Who filled the order?				The visitor was *who?*		

Whom is an object case pronoun corresponding to *him* or *them*. Its correctness in a sentence can be checked by the substitution of *him* or *them:*

S	V	O			OP
		(them)			(them)
The attorney advised *whom?*				The room was occupied by *whom?*	

Some sentences contain two sentence patterns. One expresses the main thought and the other expresses a related but secondary thought. Identifying the sentence patterns will reveal whether *who* or *whom* is required in the secondary pattern:

Roger Terrell is the grocer (who, whom) we contacted.

     s   LV   CN
Roger Terrell is the grocer
(s)   (v)   (o)
we contacted (who, whom)

Notice the analysis of the following examples:

The man (who, whom) can advise you is Howard Beals.

    s LV   CN   (s)   (v)   (o)
The man is Howard Beals   (who, whom) can advise you

We were delighted with the woman against (who, whom) we played.

    s   v   OP   (s) (v)   (OP)
We were delighted with the woman   we played against (who, whom)

After a linking verb, remember to use a subject case pronoun as a complement:

                    (s) (LV) (CP)
Did Winifred say who it had been?   (it had been he)

All that has been said about *who* and *whom* applies also to *whoever* and *whomever*. *Whoever* is a subject case pronoun and *whomever* is an object case pronoun. However, there is one point regarding their use that needs pinpointing: if both subject and object parts of sentence patterns are missing, then the pronoun chosen must be the subject, which serves a stronger function:

    s   v   (s)   (o)   (v) (o)
This firm will promote (*whoever*, whomever) serves it well.

A quick analysis into patterns reveals an object missing after "firm will promote" and also a subject missing for "serves it well." In this situation the subject function is the more important one. *Whoever* is the correct form. When you come to a study of noun clauses, you will find another explanation for the correctness of *whoever* in this construction.

If an object case pronoun is required in both sentence patterns, then *whomever* is obviously the correct form:

    s   v   OP (o) (s)   (v)
Mr. Burke works with (whoever, *whomever*) we appoint.

Complete Work Project 10

PRONOUN-ANTECEDENT AGREEMENT

A pronoun must agree with its antecedent in person, number, and gender:

The stamp *pad* had lost *its* former usefulness.

Mr. Rose and I agreed on *our* advertising layout.

Marie, please lend me *your* eraser.

Note. Errors in gender are uncommon, but keep in mind the following distinctions: people are referred to by *who* or *that;* animals and things, by *that* or *which*.

The policeman described the shoplifter *that* got away.

Everyone applauded the man *who* made the announcement.

The two cases of corned beef *that* were damaged were unusable.

The animals *which* were injured soon recovered.

Avoid: Choose as your helper a man ~~which~~ you like.

Special Problems of Pronoun-Antecedent Agreement

- A *collective noun* such as *group, staff,* or *committee* requires a singular or plural pronoun depending on whether (1) the group acts as a single unit or (2) the group acts according to the separate members within it:

  The *faculty* held *its* first meeting of the new term.

  The *staff* rushed through *its* agenda quickly.

  But

  The *faculty* have returned from *their* summer vacations.

  The *staff* differed in *their* reactions to the proposed amalgamation.

- These antecedents are singular and require a pronoun in the singular form: *anyone, anybody, a person, each, either, neither, someone, somebody, no one, nobody, everyone, everybody, many a:*

  A *person* cannot always discern *his* own progress.

  Either of the comptometer operators can add this work to *his* schedule today.

  Nobody is free to leave until *he* has finished *his* work.

  Many a career girl has changed *her* mind about marriage.

  Each of the men guaranteed *his* work.

Note.   When one of the singular antecedents cited above is not limited to either sex, then the masculine form is used:

  Somebody left *his* pocket dictionary on the table.

  No one in the audience could hold *his* laughter.

  But

  Each of the men listed *his* specialty.

  Neither of the girls heard *her* named called.

  Avoid: *Each* civilian was requested to file *his* ~~or her~~ name.

- The modern trend is to use *both, few, all, many, several, some,* and *none* as plural antecedent requiring a plural pronoun:

  None of the pickets have returned to *their* jobs.

  Some of us can reserve *our* questions for this evening's panel.

  Both the orchestras exhibited *their* conductors' skill.

When *all, some,* and *none* are used to express quantity, their meaning is singular:

  None of the thought had lost *its* originality.

  Some of the food had lost *its* appeal in transit.

  All the energy was returned to *its* former source.

- Two singular antecedents joined by *and* require a plural pronoun:

  The *foreman* and his *assistant* shared *their* information.

If two singular antecedents joined by *and* identify the same person or thing, then a singular pronoun is used:

  The *president* and *chairman* of the board presented *his* analysis of the crisis.

- When *each, every,* or *no* precede two singular antecedents, the pronoun is singular:

  Each letter and report makes *its* own special demand on the writer.

  Every tool and die has *its* own number.

  No apology and *no* explanation has found *its* way to my desk as yet.

- In a *who* construction, be sure to make the pronoun agree with the true antecedent:

  Sharon is one of the *women* who have donated *their* blood.
    (Sharon is one of what group? *Women* who have donated *their* blood.)

  Mr. Andrews is one of those *people* who refuse to admit *their* limitations.
    (Mr. Andrews is one of what group? *People* who refuse to admit *their* limitations.)

  Albert is the only *one* of the executives who can type *his* own letters.
    (Albert is one of which group? None. *Only* Albert can type *his* own letters.)

- When a singular and a plural antecedant are connected by *or* or *nor*, the plural antecedent is placed last and the pronoun is made plural:

  The receptionist or the other *girls* will share *their* stationery with you.

  Neither the treasurer nor his *assistants* could locate *their* mistake.

- Nouns introduced by *as well as, together with,* and *in addition to* cannot serve as antecedents:

  Junior Price, as well as his wife, expressed *his* gratitude.

  The *passengers*, in addition to the driver, yelled *their* objections.

- Avoid a weak pronoun reference. Every antecedent must have a clearcut antecedent or else the sentence should be rewritten:

  The factory lost another valuable day of production. *This* was expensive.
    (This delay was expensive.)

  We were all asked to offer suggestions, *which* we can do.
    (We can all comply with this request.)

  We were all asked to offer suggestions. *This* we can all do.
    (We can all comply with this request.)

Complete Work Projects 11-13

WORK PROJECT 9

Pronoun Function and Pronoun Case

A.   Draw an arrow from each pronoun to its antecedent.

Ex: Thornton summoned his secretary for her advice.

1.   The stock market registered its highest loss of the season today.

2.   Mr. Forbes and his son helped themselves to more food.

3.   The rancher gave up his claim to the mineral rights.

4.   Jeannette bought the geranium because it reminded her of her mother.

5.   I picked up my books and went to my room.

6.   The tourists greeted the Mexicans and thanked them for their

hospitality.

7.   Jane smiled as she took the ring and placed it on her finger.

8.   The tank exploded, and it spread its contents all over the building.

9.   Sinclair and I ourselves prepared the batter for the waffles.

10.   The architect asked the contractors to notify him of any changes

in their materials.

B.   Underline each pronoun in the following sentence and identify its function.

          s   o
Ex: He saw her last night.

                  OP   CP
The man with her was he.

1.   We conducted ourselves like gentlemen.

2.   He and the engineer disagreed about it.

3.   The disguise fooled them temporarily.

4. It was she on the telephone.

5. The wardrobe mistress had ironed it for her.

6. We left a note for him.

7. They and ten other members bought it for him.

8. The valedictorian was he.

9. They told her too soon.

10. The suit was filed by him and her.

C. Eliminating errors in pronoun case. Choose the correct form in the following sentences and write it in the space at the right. When in doubt, prove your answer by filling in the sentence pattern. Any pronoun left over will have to be an object of a preposition.

Ex: The doctor questioned Ronald and (he, him) about the food. ....him............

      s   v   o

(He, Him) and his neighbors enjoy their privacy. ....He............

1. The patrolman asked Paul and (I, me) for our licenses. ....

2. Both of (us, we) girls wanted the invitation. ....

3. The position challenged him more than (I, me). ....

4. Mr. Bradley and (she, her) argued on our side. ....

5. (We, Us) union members have negotiated a contract. ....

6. The receipts were issued by Miss Tanner and (I, me). ....

7. The losers were the mayor and (they, them). ....

8. Between Bart and (she, her), the matter was settled. ....

9. Richard, don't (we, us) veterans get first choice? ....

10. Who played against Walter and (he, him)? ....

11. (He, Him) and the trumpet player were brothers. ....

12. The man in charge of (we, us) trainees is very patient. ....

13. It was (she, her) in the cafeteria at lunch time. ....

14. He expected the help of the president and (we, us) other officials. ....

15. My husband makes better salads than (I, me). ....

16. The experienced buyers were Jack and (he, him). ....

17. The money was collected from the office staff and (he, him). ....

18. (Her, She) and Wilbert and Ann sent flowers. ....

19. Who is as efficient as (her, she)? ....

20. No one knows Mr. Copes and (she, her) very well. ....

WORK PROJECT 10

Using -self Words, Who-Whom, and Whoever-Whomever

A. Write in the correct form in the space provided at the right.

1. The chairman and the secretary and (myself, I) arranged the conference. ....

2. Mr. Hawkins (hisself, himself) joked with us. ....

3. The packers preferred to eat lunch by (theirselves, themselves). ....

4. Those three fellows have confidence in (themself, themselves, theirself, theirselves). ....

5. Many other group leaders and (myself, I) had our hands full with the boys. ....

6. The first choices were Miss Perkins and (I, myself). ....

7. The Martins and I bet against (ourself, ourselves). ....

8. The three sorriest-looking specimens were Beaumont, Parker, and (myself, I). ....

9. Henry first chastized (hisself, himself). ....

10. We were instructed to decide on a schedule for (ourself, ourselves). ....

B. In the space provided below compose two sentences around each -*self* word in parentheses. In the first sentence use the -*self* word to emphasize and in the second to refer the action back to the subject.

Ex: (yourself)   You yourself saw what happened.

   You didn't fool yourself very long.

1. (herself)   ....

   ....

2. (itself)   ....

   ....

3. (ourselves)   ....

   ....

4. (myself) ....

....

5. (themselves) ....

....

C. Write the correct form in the space provided at the right. When in doubt, write in above the word in parentheses the other pronoun form that proves your answer (he, him, etc.). In some instances you will need to fill in the basic sentence patterns.

```
                    o        s      v
                  (him)
Ex:  (Who, Whom)  do   you   recommend?                    whom

     (s)                  s     v         (v)
     (Who, Whom)  do   you   believe   could   qualify?     who
```

1. (Who, Whom) did you speak with yesterday? ....

2. (Who, Whom) did you telephone? ....

3. (Who, Whom) were the auditors? ....

4. The remnants were shipped to (who, whom)? ....

5. (Who, Whom) had he offended? ....

6. The woman (who, whom) entered was my cousin. ....

7. The man (who, whom) you interviewed was the owner. ....

8. The home company will announce (who, whom) has been promoted. ....

9. Miss Cobb listed the girls (who, whom) the agency had employed. ....

10. Did he know (who, whom) it was? ....

11. (Who, Whom) did you say called? ....

12. The attorney (who, whom) we congratulated won the case. ....

13. We rented the trailer to a man (who, whom) we already knew. ....

14. Please suggest (whoever, whomever) you like. ....

15. Give this advertising material to (whoever, whomever) requests it. ....

16. The winner of the sales contest will be (whoever, whomever) gets the MacPherson order. ....

17. (Who, Whom) do you think borrowed my stylus? ....

18. More precautions should be taken by (whoever, whomever) operates the power motor.   ....

19. Mrs. Moore is a friend to (whoever, whomever) she likes.   ....

20. Mr. Sanders will probably approve (whoever, whomever) we send.   ....

21. With (who, whom) has he been corresponding?   ....

22. She knew (who, whom) I had recommended.   ....

23. Additional supplies will be issued to (whoever, whomever) needs them.   ....

24. (Who, Whom) can we request the information from?   ....

25. There were only ten applicants (who, whom) we could hire.   ....

26. Mr. Edgars talked to a man (who, whom) had graduated recently.   ....

27. This product will please the customers for (who, whom) it was designed.   ....

28. The envelope was mistakenly addressed to (who, whom)?   ....

29. Mrs. Sullivan is the accountant (who, whom) handles such matters.   ....

30. Allen is one of the four men (who, whom) we recently promoted.   ....

WORK PROJECT 11

Eliminating Errors in Pronoun-Antecedent Agreement

Write the correct form in the space provided at the right.

1. The team bought corsages for (its, their) girlfriends. ....

2. Many an erring husband has told (his, their) wife that story! ....

3. No one knew where (he, they) had seen him. ....

4. Each of the office boys offered (his, their) assistance. ....

5. The foreman of the jury arose to announce (its, their) verdict. ....

6. Someone wrote (his, their) telephone number on this pad. ....

7. Each office member was asked to make (his, their, his or her) contribution to the Christmas fund. ....

8. Either of the clerks can give you (his, their) help. ....

9. None of the visitors have given us (his, their) reactions. ....

10. Margaret is one of those women who devote much energy to (her, their) favorite charities. ....

11. Each officer and member pays (his, their) own expenses. ....

12. The notorious forger and embezzler threw (himself, themselves) on the mercy of the court. ....

13. Mr. Burns is the only one of the agents who will return (his, their) receipts. ....

14. The checker or the packagers will lend you (his, their) help. ....

15. My son, as well as his friend, gave me (his, their) word. ....

16. Either of the fellows can train you in (his, their) routine. ....

17. No carpenter and no plumber arrived to take (his, their) place on the panel. ....

18. Everyone likes to see (his, their) name in print. ....

19. Tina, together with the older woman, let us know (her, their) views on the subject. ....

20. The secretary and treasurer of the firm submitted (his, their) annual resignation! ....

WORK PROJECT 12

Eliminating Vague Pronoun References

In the space provided, rewrite the following sentences to eliminate the weak reference of pronouns.

Ex: Janice frequently speaks in a high-pitched voice, which bothers her.

Janice frequently speaks in a high-pitched voice, a tendency which bothers her.

Normally we wash and cull the fruit but ship it unrefrigerated. This has been acceptable to the wholesalers.

Normally we wash and cull the fruit but ship it unrefrigerated. This practice has been acceptable

to the wholesalers.

1. The contract stipulated that the rent should begin in three months. We agreed to that.

....

....

2. Our products are always attractively packaged and displayed, which explains their success.

....

....

3. Twice during the last month we have had to cancel the Saturday afternoon performance. Is this unavoidable?

....

....

4. If we can cut down on production costs by two per cent, then we can compete favorably with rival firms, which will please J. B.

....

....

5. The division manager said, "Every item we carry in stock should be subject to a continual inventory." I agree with this.

....

....

WORK PROJECT 13

Correcting Copy with Mistakes in the Use of Pronouns

The following letter contains many errors in the form, person, and case of pronouns. Place a check mark (√) after the number of each line that contains one or more errors.

JUNIOR BOOSTERS INTERNATIONAL

Alman Building   101 Chancery Street   Medford, Ohio

June 3, 19—

Mr. J. Sutton Jones, Director

Junior Boosters International

1677 Northfield Drive

Memphis, Tennessee

Dear Jack

SUBJECT: The Hong Kong Conference

Roger Banks and myself have just returned from a highly   1 ....

profitable tour of the Far East and—in general—can report a   2 ....

growing interest in the JBI movement. The plans for the Hong   3 ....

Kong conference are definitely set, and both Roger and me were   4 ....

impressed with the determination of the Hong Kong chapter to   5 ....

make this a memorable occasion.   6 ....

      At the first Conference Committee meeting, each of the partici-   7 ....
pants was asked to give their suggestion for a conference theme.   8 ....
Most of the ideas advanced seemed unimaginative to Roger and I   9 ....
and also to Mr. Ah Wong, who, as president of the local chapter   10 ....
and chairman of the committee, said that each general convoca-   11 ....
tion and panel discussion should advance some aspect of a vital   12 ....
idea. That vital idea was finally supplied by Mr. Leonardo   13 ....
Badar, a Filipino lawyer on an extended business assignment in   14 ....
Hong Kong. He is one of those men who became successful   15 ....
entirely on his own merits—the pattern admired by so many of   16 ....
we Americans.   17 ....

      He was skeptical of conferences which attempted to explore too   18 ....
broad a theme; in the past, he argued, many a delegate had gone   19 ....
home with no clearcut idea about how to help their local com-   20 ....
munity. Since the avowed goal of our organization is leader-   21 ....
ship training of young men at the local level, he felt that the   22 ....
group should concentrate its efforts on specific plans for   23 ....
building recreation centers, child-care clinics, and libraries.   24 ....
With refreshing candor he pointed out that outright gifts of   25 ....
these things from Americans had often created hostility in the   26 ....
recipients and bewilderment or anger in the donors. The   27 ....
reason: people in the receiving community felt themself un-   28 ....
involved in their own improvement. They were the "less fortu-   29 ....
nate" who were expected to appreciate an act of charity. If   30 ....
the older, more established JBI chapters would supply the plans,   31 ....
the tools, and some supervisory know-how, then he felt the   32 ....
backward communities would be proud to do their share by   33 ....
supplying the raw materials and the labor. This, he was con-   34 ....
vinced, would engender mutual respect besides providing a   35 ....
meaningful experience in leadership training.   36 ....

Mr. Wong, as well as the others, gave their approval to this   37 ....

suggestion for a conference theme. An outline of the confer-   38 ....

ence will be mailed to you shortly. Please let me have your   39 ....

reaction to it so that I can publicize the conference in all   40 ....

JBI publications.   41 ....

    Mr. Badar is the kind of young man who we need in a key   42 ....

position, don't you agree?   43 ....

Cordially yours

JUNIOR BOOSTERS INTERNATIONAL

Philip Wilkerson

Philip Wilkerson
Secretary General

mn

In the spaces provided below, first list the number of the line which contains error(s). Then supply the correction(s) in the other spaces.

Ex: ....1.... ....Banks and I................ ....

....

....

....

....

....

....

....

....

....

....

....

7 VERBS

Verbs are the workhorses of our language. They carry the burden of getting across our thoughts about the things we single out for attention. An effective choice of verbs spurs our thoughts across the page in swift, vivid strides. One surefooted verb can often deliver our meaning more economically than a sentenceful of modifying words and constructions:

> He *scribbled* the note.
>
> (He wrote the note in a manner that was not immediately decipherable and denoted undue speed or haste.)

How Verbs Can Help You Improve Your Writing Proficiency

Teaching you how to choose verbs effectively is, of course, outside the scope of this book. What we are concerned with is the correctness of the verb once you have chosen it. Does it operate properly in its relationship to other words? Does it fit the right subject? Does it convey the precise time component of the action or possession or state of being?

Largely this section on verbs has been designed to review for you only those aspects that habitually cause trouble. Surprisingly, an attempt to analyze verbs too fully can often result in the temporary loss of a student's native grasp of the matter. Self-consciousness sets in, and he may begin making errors where formerly there were none.

You already know how to use most verbs correctly. We will concentrate on sensitive areas: irregular verbs, special uses of perfect tenses, and subject-verb agreement. Verb errors are often called "sore-thumbs" because they stick out. Eliminating them is a "must" if you are to convey to others an impression of a good educational background.

THE FUNCTIONS OF VERBS

Verbs were originally defined in Section I as words asserting action (He *spoke*), possession (He *had* it), or state of being (He *was* ready). This definition identifies verbs on the basis of meaning or function. It is possible, however, to determine a verb by its position in a sentence in relation to other words. A quick glance at the basic sentence patterns will refresh your memory:

S   V
Mr. Cole retired.

S   V   O
She typed the memorandum.

S   LV   CN
Helen is the expert.

S LV CP
It is she.

S   LV   CA
She is efficient.

Obviously, a verb or linking verb normally follows its subject and precedes any object or complement. This principle applies even though modifying constructions are applied to the subject:

S   V
The man in the Santa Claus suit smiled.

S   V   O
One of the women in the crowd signaled the auctioneer.

S   LV   CN
The clerk at the desk by the window is Marsden Price.

VERB TENSE

Tense, the main characteristic of a verb, indicates the time of the action or possession or state of being. We measure tense from the moment of speaking, which is considered to be the present:

PAST	PRESENT	FUTURE
Yesterday he *spoke*. (time before the moment of speaking or writing)	Today he *speaks*. (moment of speaking or writing)	Tomorrow he *will speak*. (time after moment of speaking or writing)

The three verbs in the sentences above illustrate what are called simple or uncomplicated tenses. Often, however, we need to know whether an action being referred to a specified point of time was completed before that time (*perfect* tense) or whether an action continues or progresses beyond the specified time (*progressive* tense).

All verbs are derived from what is called the infinitive form or name of the verb. For instance, *am, are, is, was,* and so on are verb forms derived from the infinitive *to be;* and *begin, began, has begun, will begin,* and so on are derived from the infinitive *to begin.* The sign of an infinitive is *to.*

Because the infinitive form, *to sell,* does not limit the action to a person or time or number, we cannot say

Mary *to sell* rugs.

We would have to say

Mary *sells* rugs.

Mary *has sold* rugs.

The following is an illustration of the simple tense verbs that are derived from the infinitive *to walk.* Each form, you will notice, is limited in person, number, and tense:

NUMBER	PERSON	PRESENT TENSE	PAST TENSE	FUTURE TENSE
	1. (I)	walk	walked	will walk
SINGULAR	2. (you)	walk	walked	will walk
	3. (he)	walks	walked	will walk
	1. (we)	walk	walked	will walk
PLURAL	2. (you)	walk	walked	will walk
	3. (they)	walk	walked	will walk

Note. Though some grammarians still insist on distinguishing between *shall* and *will*, most Americans altogether ignore it. However, an older generation of business people may require it of you. In that case, use *shall* with *I* and *we* to express the future tense; reverse the use to express determination:

Futurity:

(I, We) shall arrive tomorrow.
(You, He, She, It, They) will arrive tomorrow.

Determination:

(I, We) will fight until the ammunition gives out.
(You, He, She, They) shall stay in jail until Wednesday.

As the chart on page 70 indicates, there are also forms for the present progressive and present perfect tenses, etc. Here again your native grasp of language comes in to make it unnecessary for you to memorize all the given forms of a particular verb. It is sufficient for you to know only what is called the *principal parts* of a verb—the first person forms for the present, the past, and the past participle. Study the chart on page 70 carefully, being sure to test these points of emphasis:

• All forms of the present tense are the same for all three persons, singular and plural, except the third person singular form, which always ends in *s*.

MAIN TENSES OR TIMES

KIND OF ACTION	PRESENT	PAST	FUTURE
SIMPLE	I *work*. (general action in present time) The rain in Spain *stays* mainly in the plain. (habitual or relatively permanent action)	I *worked*. (action in past which was definitely completed)	I *will work*. (action to take place at a future time)
PROGRESSIVE (action continuing beyond time indicated)	I *am working* in the kitchen. (action in progress at moment of speaking or writing)	I *was working* when the telephone rang. (definite action in past which was incompleted or interrupted)	I *will be working*. (action to take place in future, with emphasis on the continuing nature of the action)
PERFECT (action completed or perfected prior to the time indicated)	I *have worked* at many jobs. (action completed at some indefinite past time) I *have worked* for an hour. (action begun in the past which has continued to the moment of speaking or writing)	I *had worked* as a soda jerker before I entered the service. (past action which was completed before another past action or time)	At noon tomorrow I *will have worked* in this office for ten years. (future action which will be completed before another future action or time)

TO ENJOY

	PRESENT			PAST	PAST PARTICIPLE
PRINCIPAL PARTS	ENJOY			ENJOYED	ENJOYED
Present	*Present progressive*	*Future*		*Past*	*Present Perfect*
1. enjoy	1. am enjoying	1. will enjoy		1. enjoyed	1. have enjoyed
2. enjoy	2. are enjoying	2. will enjoy		2. enjoyed	2. have enjoyed
3. enjoys	3. is enjoying	3. will enjoy		3. enjoyed	3. has enjoyed
1. enjoy	1. are enjoying	1. will enjoy		1. enjoyed	1. have enjoyed
2. enjoy	2. are enjoying	2. will enjoy		2. enjoyed	2. have enjoyed
3. enjoy	3. are enjoying	3. will enjoy		3. enjoyed	3. have enjoyed

TO SPEAK

	PRESENT			PAST	PAST PARTICIPLE
PRINCIPAL PARTS	SPEAK			SPOKE	SPOKEN
Present	*Present Progressive*	*Future*		*Past*	*Present Perfect*
1. speak	1. am speaking	1. will speak		1. spoke	1. have spoken
2. speak	2. are speaking	2. will speak		2. spoke	2. have spoken
3. speaks	3. is speaking	3. will speak		3. spoke	3. has spoken
1. speak	1. are speaking	1. will speak		1. spoke	1. have spoken
2. speak	2. are speaking	2. will speak		2. spoke	2. have spoken
3. speak	3. are speaking	3. will speak		3. spoke	3. have spoken

• All forms for the past tense and the future tense are the same.

• All forms made with the present and past participles are the same except for the helping words. A participle is not a tense; it is the verb form used with helping words such as *is* and *have* (*is working, have worked*). Present participles, which show that an action continues beyond the time of beginning, are made up of the present form plus *-ing*. Past participles simply have to be known for each verb, though normally the past participle is the same as the form used for the past tense: He *has worked*.

REGULAR VERBS

Verbs like *to walk* are called *regular* because they form the past and past participle by adding *-ed* to the present form. Some regular verbs end in *t* or *d: slept, fired*. All but a handful of English verbs are regular and present no problems in using the correct form:

INFINITIVE	PRESENT	PAST	PAST PARTICIPLE
to operate	operate	operated	operated
to hire	hire	hired	hired
to keep	keep	kept	kept
to change	change	changed	changed
to caution	caution	cautioned	cautioned

IRREGULAR VERBS

To begin is called an *irregular verb* because it forms the past and past participle in a radical manner (*began, begun*). Though there are approximately two hundred of these irregular verbs in English, they do not give us quite as much difficulty as might be anticipated. Chiefly they are everyday verbs. Even so, most people trip over a few of them. Read through the following list carefully, testing yourself as you do. Be sure to note your own difficulties.

bear	bore	borne
beat	beat	beaten
begin	began	begun
bite	bit	bitten
blow	blew	blown
burst	burst	burst
choose	chose	chosen
cling	clung	clung
come	came	come
drag	dragged	dragged
drink	drank	drunk
drive	drove	driven
do	did	done
draw	drew	drawn
eat	ate	eaten
fly	flew	flown
fall	fell	fallen
forecast	forecast	forecast
forget	forgot	forgotten (forgot)
forsake	forsook	forsaken
freeze	froze	frozen
get	got	got (gotten)
give	gave	given
go	went	gone
grind	ground	ground
grow	grew	grown
hang (an object)	hung	hung
But: hang (a person)	hanged	hanged (a regular verb)
hit	hit	hit
know	knew	known
lead	led	led
meet	met	met
mean	meant	meant
ring	rang	rung
run	ran	run
see	saw	seen
seek	sought	sought
sew	sewed	sewed (sewn)
shake	shook	shaken
shed	shed	shed
shine (to give off light)	shone	shone
shine (to give a polish to)	shined	shined
shrink	shrank (shrunk)	shrunk (shrunken)
sink	sank (sunk)	sunk
sing	sang	sung
slay	slew	slain
speak	spoke	spoken

spring	sprang (sprung)	sprung
sting	stung	stung
swear	swore	sworn
swim	swam	swum
swing	swung	swung
take	took	taken
teach	taught	taught
tear	tore	torn
throw	threw	thrown
wake	waked (woke)	waked (woken)
wear	wore	worn
write	wrote	written

To be is so irregular that even the forms in the present and past are not consistent throughout:

1.	am	1.	was	1.	been
2.	are	2.	were	2.	been
3.	is	3.	was	3.	been
1.	are	1.	were	1.	been
2.	are	2.	were	2.	been
3.	are	3.	were	3.	been

Complete Work Project 14

LIE, LAY; SIT, SET; RISE, RAISE

These three pairs of irregular verbs cause a good deal of confusion and therefore merit special consideration.

INFINITIVE	PRESENT	PAST	PAST PARTICIPLE
to lie (to recline)	lie	lay	lain
to lay (to place)	lay	laid	laid
to sit (to occupy a seat)	sit	sat	sat
to set (to place)	set	set	set
to rise (to get up or lift up)	rise	rose	risen
to raise (to lift another object or to cause it to rise)	raise	raised	raised

Applying the sentence patterns will prevent errors in choosing the correct forms of these verbs. *Rise, lie,* and *sit* will occur in the first sentence pattern:

s	v	
The market price	rose	sharply yesterday.
John	has sat	down.
She	lies	down on the office couch.

Raise, lay, and *set* will occur in the second sentence pattern:

s	v	o	
The custodian	raised	the window.	
He	lays	the letters	in my box.
Mr. Hines	has set	the pace	for the salesmen.

Another way to help discern which verb to use is to substitute *place* for *lay* or *set:*

(placed)
Mr. Hall laid the checks on the counter.

(~~placing~~)
He was lying there fast asleep.   (He was not placing anything; there is no object to receive the action, and the verb is therefore *lying.*)

Complete Work Project 15

SUBJECT-VERB AGREEMENT

A native speaker of English automatically makes a verb agree with its subject in person (first, second, third) and in number (singular or plural). However, several kinds of subject-verb agreement need special emphasis. The following sentences can be used as study guides for determining the correct verb form in problem situations:

1. Jerry or Albert (assemble, *assembles*) the materials.

2. Mr. Olivier or his daughters (has, *have*) translated the novel.

3. His daughters or Mr. Olivier himself (*has,* have) translated the novel.

4. Either the switch or the lever (*is,* are) not functioning correctly.

5. Neither Roberts & Rinehart nor the other companies (*offer,* offers) much chance for advancement just now.
   Note. In these situations, *or* and *nor* are separating words; the verb agrees with the subject nearest it. It is an excellent idea to re-cast sentences such as these:
   Neither the timekeeper nor the clerks (*contribute,* contributes) to the coffee fund.
   (The timekeeper does not contribute to the coffee fund, and neither do the clerks.)

6. Mr. Burns and Mr. Taylor (*dictate,* dictates) very rapidly.
   Note. The *and* makes a plural subject.

7. Electronics (*is,* are) an expanding field.
   Note. *Electronics* is a singular word, even though it ends in *s.*

8. The geological phenomena (is, *are*) a challenge to our ingenuity.
   Note. *Phenomena* is a borrowed word for which the foreign plural is maintained.

9. There (was, *were*) several reasons for his optimism.

10. There (*lie,* lies) the requisitions for this department.
    Note. The subjects, which are plural, come after the verb.

11. One of the girls (*has,* have) had experience in preparing income tax forms.
    Note. *One* is the subject of the sentence; since it is already serving as the object of a preposition, *girls* cannot influence the verb.

12. Nancy, as well as Norma, (like, *likes*) to gossip.
    Nancy, in addition to Norma,
    Nancy, no less than Norma,
    Nancy, together with Norma,
    Note. In each of these sentences, *Norma* is part of the parenthetical material and is not free to affect the verb. The commas are clues that the group of words ending in *Norma* interrupts the normal subject-verb order and that *Norma* is therefore not part of the subject.

13. The company team (lose, *loses*) almost every game.

14. The company team (*take*, takes) their wives with them to the games.

15. A number of people (is, *are*) going to the resort for the holiday.

16. The number of tourists (*is*, are) increasing each year.
     Note. Is the group being referred to as a single unit or as a group of separately acting individuals? Remember this simple rule: *a number . . . are, the number . . . is.*

17. Mr. Horner is a man who (cling, *clings*) to tradition.

18. Mr. Horner is one of those people who (*cling*, clings) to tradition .

19. Mr. Horner is the *only* one of the men who (sing, *sings*) in a choir.
     Note. In sentence 17, *who* is singular because it relates to *man;* in sentence 18, *who* is plural because it relates to *people;* in sentence 19, the word *only* means that *who* must relate to *one*, not to *men.*

20. Thirty dollars *is* a good wholesale price for that item.

21. An hour and thirty minutes *is* a long time to wait.

22. Six months *was* the time stipulated in the contract.

23. Four yards *is* half the amount on hand.
     Note. Quantities and sums or multiples of numbers express a singular idea and require a singular verb.

24. The truck and trailer *was* correctly parked.

25. A mayor and former congressman *has agreed* to speak.

26. Peaches and cream *is* a delectable dessert.
     Note. In these sentences the compound subjects identify the same person or thing, and thus the verb is singular.

27. Each knife, fork, and spoon *was* placed properly on the table.

28. Every man and woman *is* subject to the new ruling.

29. Many a stockholder and investor *takes* the path of least resistance.
     Note. Subjects connected by *and* but preceded by the distinguishing words *each, every*, or *many a* convey a singular meaning.

30. Our own planning, not the mistakes of our opponents, *has won* the election for us.
     Note. *Mistakes*, the noun used in the contrast, does not influence the verb. It agrees with the subject *planning*, which is used affirmatively.

Complete Work Project 16

SOME SPECIAL USES OF TENSE

Though errors in tense are infrequently made, some uses of tenses need extra emphasis, especially the perfect tenses.

The *present perfect* tense is used to show a past action or state continuing into the present (the moment of speaking or writing):

Present: Mr. Carey *is* my boss.

Past: Mr. Carey *was* my boss.   (He fired me.)

Present perfect: Mr. Carey *has been* my boss for three years. (He began being my boss three years ago and he still is at the present moment.)

Another use of the present perfect tense is to indicate that an action has been completed at some indefinite time in the past:

Past: Yesterday the mail *arrived* at ten o'clock.

Present perfect: The mail *has arrived.* (indefinite past time)

The *past perfect* tense is used to show, with respect to past time, that one thing happened before another:

Miss Chin realized that she *had typed* the wrong quotation.
(Typing the quotation took place before the action of realizing that fact)

Use the present tense for statements permanently true:

He felt that youth *is* wasted on the young.

We fished on White River, which *is* in the Ozarks.

THE SUBJUNCTIVE MOOD

The subjunctive mood is rapidly disappearing, though it is most regularly retained to express conditions contrary to fact and to indicate doubt, regret, or a wish:

If I *were* you, I would leave on the early plane.

I wish that I *were* going, too.

That gladiolus looks as if it *were* diseased.

Complete Work Projects 17 and 18

WORK PROJECT 14

Using the Correct Form of Irregular Verbs

A. Write the correct form in the space at the right.

1. That company has (flew, flown) six million passenger miles without incident. ....

2. Hundreds of bells (rang, rung) in the new year. ....

3. Our firm has (born, borne, bore) the heavy research costs for years without raising prices. ....

4. She (begun, began) to feel better almost immediately. ....

5. One of the machines (grinded, ground) the glass into a fine powder. ....

6. Three days have (went, gone) by since Gary's prediction of a price war. ....

7. What (lead, led) you to that conclusion, Bill? ....

8. The front door (swang, swung) back and forth continually. ....

9. The roof has (sprang, sprung) no more leaks during the rainy season. ....

10. One foreign government has (froze, frozen) the assets of American investors. ....

11. Anyone who sends his mother a greeting card like that should be (hanged, hung)! ....

12. Has good weather been (forcast, forecast, forecasted, forcasted) for tomorrow? ....

13. He (drunk, drank) enough water to quench the thirst of a horse. ....

14. That piece of plywood will (bust, burst) under all that weight. ....

15. Have the members (chose, chosen) the meeting place? ....

16. They might have (did, done) the work by themselves. ....

17. The boat had (tore, torn) away from the mooring. ....

18. One of the maids had (woke, woken) me with her vacuuming. ....

19. Where has the wasp (stang, stung) you? ....

20. How much money have you (sank, sunk) into bonds? ....

21. The vigilantes caught and (hung, hanged) three desperadoes within a week. ....

22. We have grown so much the past year that we have (burst, busted) out of our original building! ....

23. Winifred (chose, choosed) to go straight home.

....

24. The raccoon had (bit, bitten) through the leather thong on the door of the trap.

....

....

25. Mr. Olds had (spoken, spoke) straight from the shoulder.

....

26. Have they (written, wrote) their fathers recently?

....

27. At long last I had (come, came) to the end of the tape.

....

28. No one noticed where the package had (fallen, fell).

....

29. Who did you say had (stolen, stole) your idea?

....

30. All that money sat there temptingly, but Homer (clung, clang) to his honor.

....

B. Incorporate each of the following verb forms into a sentence.

1. burst (past tense) ....

....

2. run (past participle) ....

....

3. shone (past participle) ....

....

4. dragged (past tense) ....

....

5. forsaken ....

....

6. hung (past tense) ....

....

WORK PROJECT 15

Using the Correct Form of Irregular Verbs

A. Underline the correct form of the verb in parentheses. Prove your answer by identifying the sentence patterns and by substituting appropriate forms of *to place* for *lay* and *set*.

<pre>
         S   V
Ex: He has (laid, lain) there too long.
         S   V(placed)   O
     Mr. Suttle has (laid, lain) the matter before us clearly.
</pre>

1. (Set, Sit) down on the chair and behave yourself, Timothy Newton.

2. I can't remember when prices have (raised, risen) so sharply.

3. She just (sits, sets) there and stares at her shorthand pad.

4. Richard (laid, lay) awake all night and pondered what to do.

5. Mr. Murchison (raised, rose) his hand in greeting.

6. The missing cover has (laid, lain) there on the floor for months.

7. The vegetables have (set, sat) in the sun too long.

8. The temperature will have (risen, raised) ten degrees by nine o'clock.

9. Have you (set, sat) by the window and watched the leaves fall?

10. The visitors are (sitting, setting) in the waiting room.

11. He (lies, lays) down for a nap each time he finishes a campus tour.

12. The clothes had (laid, lain) on the floor all night.

13. The soufflé (raised, rose) gratifyingly and then collapsed when I opened the oven door.

14. A personal thank-you note is (laying, lying) on your desk.

15. A few men (lay, laid) alongside the pool and roasted their backs.

B. Use each of the following verb forms in a sentence.

1. lay (past tense) ....
2. lain ....
3. set (past participle) ....
4. laid (past tense) ....
5. setting ....
6. lying ....
7. lay (present tense) ....
8. laying ....
9. raised (past participle) ....
10. raised (past tense) ....

WORK PROJECT 16

Subject-Verb Agreement

Write the correct form of the verb in the space at the right.

1. Neither of the girls (take, takes) dictation. ....

2. One of the wrappers (have, has) a knife. ....

3. There (are, is) too many discrepancies in her story. ....

4. The speakers or the chairman (require, requires) the water. ....

5. There (lie, lies) the notebook and the wallet. ....

6. The staff (submit, submits) individual reports. ....

7. Which one of the panel discussions (intrigue, intrigues) you? ....

8. The girl and her mother (is, are) going to work on Sunday. ....

9. Mr. Carsten, as well as Mr. Burns (has, have) given me good advice. ....

10. Either of the calendars (is, are) attractive. ....

11. There (wasn't, weren't) many catalogs in stock. ....

12. Civics (is, are) the topic of Mr. McCall's address to the Jaycees. ....

13. The club (are, is) holding (its, their) annual breakfast meeting at the lake. ....

14. Neither the display nor the products (look, looks) appealing. ....

15. Mr. Abbott is one of the men who (like, likes) to commute in a sports car. ....

16. Ann Margaret is one of those women who never (argue, argues) with a man. ....

17. Twenty-five dollars (is, are) a lot to pay for a permanent wave! ....

18. A tax expert and former football star (join, joins) our office force in March. ....

19. Many an actress (has, have) been faced with that decision. ....

20. One of the men (is, are) happy about the publicity. ....

21. "Man Against Darkness" is the only one of the essays which (challenge, challenges) me. ....

22. Each bolt and screw (are, is) properly tightened. ....

23. Fifteen months (have, has) been the usual term of expiration on the lease. ....

24. Many a company (make, makes) the change-over without a loss. ....

25. The sister, not the brothers, (control, controls) the family investing. ....

26. Mr. Perkins, as well as his son, (like, likes) to sing in barbershop quartets. ....

27. The memoranda (is, are) lying on your desk. ....

28. The sons or the father (do, does) the hiring. ....

29. Jim, together with his family, (have, has) spent the summer in Boston. ....

30. A senator and former Rotarian (send, sends) us this literature. ....

31. He is one of the men who (join, joins) our club every other year. ....

32. Peter, no less than Paul, (have, has) an admirable background in theoretical economics. ....

33. The fungi (is, are) being forwarded to a laboratory for further research. ....

34. The committee regularly (formulate, formulates) company policy. ....

35. John Paul Jones is the only one of the customers who (object, objects) to the new billing date. ....

36. Nine times seven (is, are) sixty-three, Miss Platt. ....

37. Every boy and girl (wish, wishes) to see the show. ....

38. Either the suit or the tie (is, are) uncomplimentary to his coloring. ....

39. Neither the Whitehouse nor the Emporium (is, are) increasing the sales force. ....

40. The owner, not the manager, (has, have) shown an interest in remodeling the shipping room. ....

41. A number of our employees (is, are) studying at night school. ....

42. The herd of cattle (was, were) a good invesment. ....

43. The number of damaged articles (has, have) been sharply reduced. ....

44. Louis is one of those men who (make, makes) everything that happens a dramatic incident. ....

45. A number of packages (was, were) still awaiting delivery. ....

WORK PROJECT 17

Special Uses of Tenses and the Subjunctive Mood

A. Write in the correct form in the space at the right.

1. They (were, have been) employed since last December.　　　.....................................

2. Mr. Hope realized that he (convinced, had convinced) his boss of the need to tear out the east wall.　　　.....................................

3. By the time Christmas rolled around, Roger (became, had become) engaged again.　　　.....................................

4. If I (was, were) you, I would do the work by myself.　　　.....................................

5. Our attorney claimed he (gave, had given) us enough information to make an intelligent decision.　　　.....................................

6. For years this company (rewarded, has rewarded) its most productive employees with a bonus; the practice should be continued.　　　.....................................

7. He (did not see, has not seen) the report since last Tuesday.　　　.....................................

8. The Rogerses (appeared, have appeared) on television many times before they received good reviews.　　　.....................................

9. That poor man looks as if he (was, were) dead.　　　.....................................

10. Let's borrow Timothy's sailboat; he (owned, has owned) one for years.　　　.....................................

11. Elizabeth concluded that he (anticipated, had anticipated) her reaction.　　　.....................................

12. The perturbed young woman believed that she (offended, had offended) me.　　　.....................................

13. Mr. Johnson and his nephew (left, have left) town today.　　　.....................................

14. Cranston suspected he (failed, had failed) to make himself clear.　　　.....................................

15. He (reaffiliated, has reaffiliated) himself with his former business concern in February.　　　.....................................

16. He suggested that honesty (is, was) always the best policy.　　　.....................................

17. I (worked, have worked) diligently for two years. (Indicate that the action continues.)　　　.....................................

18. Gary (is, was) the man whom I suspect.　　　.....................................

19. Mr. Holman (was, has been) my employer for two years. (Indicate that the relationship no longer exists.)　　　.....................................

20. The mountain was nicknamed "The Skyscraper" because it (is, was) so high and steep.　　　.....................................

B. Compose sentences for the following items.

1. had succeeded° ....
....
2. has been ....
....
3. were (contrary to fact) ....
....
4. had aggravated° ....
....
5. had agreed° ....
....
6. is (in a statement permanently true) ....
....
7. had failed° ....
....
8. were (wish) ....
....
9. had disappeared° ....
....
10. has left (indefinite past time) ....
....

°Use in a sentence that describes two past actions, one a consequence of the other.

WORK PROJECT 18

Correcting Copy

The following memorandum contains many errors in the form, tense, or agreement with the subject. Place a check mark ($\sqrt{}$) after the number of each line that contains one or more errors.

INTEROFFICE MEMO

To: Paul Pierce   Date: June 12, 19—

From: Arthur Kennedy

Subject: Sales Meeting (Vacuum Cleaners)

In good faith I can report that the sales force is not	1 ....
laying down on the job. At our regular monthly sales meeting	2 ....
Friday afternoon, there was so many techniques being described	3 ....
that I had difficulty in keeping them straight. Jerry Coleman	4 ....
opened the meeting on what I had expected would be a low note:	5 ....
he reported that vacuum cleaner sales were down for the three-	6 ....
month period just ended. Harry Higgins, one of those fellows	7 ....
who always has an answer for everything, pooh-poohed the idea	8 ....
that he or the other salesmen was in any way responsible. March,	9 ....
April, and May are always poor months, he said, and forecasted	10 ....
that sales over the next three months would be the best ever.	11 ....
In my opinion four years are too short a time to establish an	12 ....
annual three-month slump, but I set there quietly because I	13 ....
didn't want to burst the balloon.	14 ....
Barney Ankers and Bert Connors plans to build good will	15 ....
for the Lady Baltimore model by emphasizing the ease with which	16 ....
it can be repaired. One of them are going to work up a half-	17 ....
page insertion for the Lady Baltimore Vacuum Cleaner Instruc-	18 ....

tion Book   (how to order parts correctly by listing the model   19 ....

number, the part number, and the part description including the   20 ....

color). Johnny Crane, together with Dick Wellband, think that   21 ....

the Power Mate attachment is the key to increased sales.   22 ....

Johnny has chose the built-in headlight as his special gimmick.   23 ....

He has rearranged the furniture in the demonstration area to   24 ....

prove to the customer that Power Mate can help her inspect   25 ....

under beds and in dark corners. Dick capitalizes on the   26 ....

recognized fact that the ideal cleaning equipment consist of   27 ....

an upright cleaner for rugs and a canister for cleaning up-   28 ....

holstered furniture, which requires a more powerful suction.   29 ....

    By the way, Harold Mosby discovered that the designer   30 ....

failed to allow enough room on the canister between the Power   31 ....

Mate hose connection and the Power Mate electrical plug. If I   32 ....

was you, I would ask him to make an oral report to Mr. Lowell.   33 ....

I know that he was qualified to make this criticism because of   34 ....

his unusual mechanical aptitude.   35 ....

A. K.

bv

In the spaces provided below, first list the number of the line which contains errors(s). Then supply the correction(s) in the other spaces.

Ex: 2   lying down   ....

   ....

   ....

   ....

   ....

   ....

   ....

   ....

   ....

   ....

8 ADJECTIVES

Adjectives are words that help us to distinguish people, places, and things from each other. They point to things near at hand or farther away, they focus attention on the characteristics of objects being identified, and they enable us to count objects being identified. When used judiciously, they add to our awareness of objects a sense of color, taste, sound, shape, size, weight, speed, and character.

How Adjectives Can Help You Improve Your Writing Proficiency

Simple as they seem, adjectives involve precise meanings and logical distinctions which the untrained person may overlook in his writing. For example, there is a good deal of difference between "*an* error" and "*the* error," and a good reason for writing "*a* huge machine" rather than "*an* huge machine." If you cannot discern what is illogical or unconventional in the following items, then a study of this unit is in order, for careful writers avoid these pitfalls in using adjectives:

less people	I can't walk any further.
the more unique design	Texas is larger than any state.
the best of two typewriters	Joe is kinder than anyone in his family.
the most unique design of all	The three clerks relieve each other
a healthy walk	for coffee breaks.
those type of clothes	I only heard him say one word.
the most loveliest woman	

IDENTIFYING ADJECTIVES

Recognizing adjectives is relatively simple if we apply the traditional questions which they answer:

Which one? *those* reports; *Mike's* wallet; her sweater

What kind? *quick* action; *Italian* food; *heavy* material

How many? *few* participants; *many* specials; *ten* questions

Both possessive nouns and possessive pronouns are considered to be adjectives because they answer the adjective question "which one?"

Ruth's schedule ended.   *His* pride was wounded.

A *proper adjective* is an adjective derived from a proper noun. It is always capitalized:

> an *English* governess, a *French* cook, a *German* car
>
> the *American* way of life

More than one adjective can occur before a noun:

> *two long* processes, *four quarrelsome old* men
>
> *several tiny brown* eggs

Word Order

An adjective can also be identified by its word order in relation to the noun or pronoun it describes:

> The *six* promoters wearing *red* badges passed out *complimentary* tickets.
> (Normally a one-word adjective occurs immediately before the noun it modifies.)

> The milk was sour.   It is his.   The money is Sam's.   He is deft.
>
> (A complement adjective occurs after the linking verb. Pronouns can be modified only by complement adjectives.)

An adjective may come after the noun if it is used in conjunction with other words or word groups:

> A woman forty pounds *lighter* stood before me.
> A (forty pounds lighter) woman. . . .

> A cause *worthy* of support is the United Crusade.
> A (worthy of support) cause. . . .

> A package four inches *shorter* would save on production costs.
> A (four inches shorter) package. . . .

Articles

A, an, and *the* are a special group of adjectives called *articles.* They are always used as adjectives. *A* and *an* are called *indefinite articles* because they are used to point out an unspecified member of a general class: *a* doctor, *an* advertisement. *The* is called a *definite* article because it distinguishes between one member and other members of a general class: *the* doctor in my ward, *the* advertisement for the apartment.

> *A* doctor usually has to work long hours.
>
> *The* doctor in my ward works long hours.
>
> *An* advertisement often gets results.
>
> *The* advertisement for the apartment brought an immediate response.

In order to maintain smooth transitions from one sound to another, it is conventional to use *a* before a noun beginning with a consonant sound (*a* walk, *a* fence, *a* dam), before a noun beginning with an *h* that is pronounced (*a* horse, *a* house), and before a noun beginning with a long *u* sound (*a* union, *a* user). *An* is used before nouns beginning with a vowel sound (*an* apple, *an* egg, *an* inlet, *an* onion, *an* ungent).

THE DEGREES OF ADJECTIVES

Notice the difference in the following uses of the adjective *quiet:*

Mr. Hawkins was a *quiet* worker.

He was *quieter* than Mr. Billings.

He was the *quietest* worker in the office.

When an adjective is used merely to describe one thing, the *positive* degree is used, as in the first sentence. When an adjective is used to show a comparison between two things, the *comparative* degree is used, as in the second sentence. When an adjective is used to show a comparison involving more than two things, the *superlative* degree is used, as in the third sentence.

The degrees of adjectives are formed in the following ways:

	POSITIVE	COMPARATIVE	SUPERLATIVE
Words of one syllable	short large	shorter larger	shortest largest
Words of two syllables, ending in *ly, er, re,* or *ow:*	lovely slender sincere narrow	lovelier slenderer sincerer narrower	loveliest slenderest sincerest narrowest
Words of two syllables, not ending in *ly, er, re,* or *ow:*	patient graceful careless	more patient more graceful more careless	most patient most graceful most careless
Words of three or more syllables:	beautiful courageous	more beautiful more courageous	most beautiful most courageous

Note 1. In general an adjective in the comparative degree is indicated by the helping word *more* or the ending *er.* The superlative degree is indicated by the helping word *most* or the ending *est.*

Note 2. The helping words *less* and *least* are used with an adjective to show lower degree:

I am not enthusiastic about that work.

I am *less* enthusiastic than Richard.   (comparative)

I am the *least* enthusiastic of all.   (superlative)

Note 3. *Unique, universal, perfect, unanimous,* and similar words cannot be used with comparative or superlative degrees. For instance, if a thing is perfect to begin with, how can it be "more perfect" or "less perfect"? By using the qualifying word *nearly,* however, we can form useful comparative and superlative degrees for these words:

POSITIVE	COMPARATIVE	SUPERLATIVE
perfect	more nearly perfect	most nearly perfect
unique	more nearly unique	most nearly unique
universal	more nearly universal	most nearly universal
unanimous	more nearly unanimous	most nearly unanimous

Here are additional words for which there are no comparative and superlative degrees without the qualifying word *nearly:*

circular	infinite	dead	round
conclusive	right	eternal	spotless
continual	immaculate	square	faultless

Adjectives Compared Irregularly

A handful of adjectives are compared irregularly. The common ones are listed below:

POSITIVE	COMPARATIVE	SUPERLATIVE
bad, ill, evil	worse	worst
far	farther	farthest
	further	furthest
good, well	better	best
late	later	latest
	latter	last
little	less, lesser	least
much, many	more	most
old	older, elder	oldest, eldest

Important Distinctions to Observe in Using the Degrees of Adjectives

Farther and *further. Farther* is preferred for referring to distance; *further,* for referring to degree or quantity:

It is *farther* to my house than to yours.

I want no *further* argument from either of you.

Further orders will be appreciated.

Later, latter, and *last. Later* denotes time; *latter* identifies the second of two items; *last* identifies the third of three items, the fourth of four items, etc.:

It is *later* than you think.

He chose the *latter* of the two alternatives.

There were suggestions to discontinue handling cosmetics, to hire a makeup consultant, and to spend more money on advertising Lady Jane products. The *last* received Mr. Mancini's approval.

Less and *fewer. Fewer* and *fewest* are used to modify nouns that emphasize number. *Less* and *least* are used to modify nouns that emphasize amount or quantity:

Fewer hours of work are required.

Less time is required.

The *fewest* tourists signed up in September.

The *least* energy is generated during the change-over.

Older, oldest; elder, eldest. Older and *oldest* are applied to persons and things. *Elder* and *eldest* apply only to people and are used to distinguish members of the same family.

Faulty comparisons. In order to avoid an illogicality, do not make a comparison like the following:

Mount Shasta is taller than any mountain in California. (Can Mount Shasta be taller than itself? More logical: Mount Shasta is taller than any *other* mountain in California.)

Miss Withers is more competent than anyone in the firm. (Can Miss Withers be more competent than herself? More logical: Miss Withers is more competent than anyone *else* in the firm.)

Complete Work Project 19

ELIMINATING USAGE ERRORS

Avoid using *them* as an adjective when *these* or *those* is called for:

He ate ~~them~~ sandwiches.   (He ate *these* [or *those*] sandwiches.)

Healthy is used to describe the state of health of a living thing; *healthful* is used to describe a thing that gives health:

We are all *healthy* men.

We are fed *healthful* food by our wives.

Avoid: I take a ~~healthy~~ walk every morning.

As adjectives, *this-these* and *that-those* are pointing words. *This* and *these* refer to things close at hand (here); *that* and *these* refer to things farther away (there):

I admire *this* picture.

How much is *that* picture at the end of the hall?

Avoid: We like this (~~here~~) book.

He sold that (~~there~~) figurine.

This and *that* agree with singular nouns; *these* and *those*, with plural nouns:

this type of clothes   those types of vegetables

Avoid: these ~~type~~ of advertisements

Each other refers to two objects; *one another*, to more than two:

They looked at *each other* like man and wife.

The entire staff agreed to remind *one another* of the new policy.

When *first* and *last* are used with adjectives expressing number, they are placed before the adjectives:

The *first* three trials won't be counted against you.

Her *last* few investments have been quite sound ones.

Only should be placed as precisely as possible:

I have *only* an hour for lunch.

Avoid: I ~~only~~ have an hour for lunch.

USING ARTICLES PRECISELY

When one noun is modified by two or more adjectives, the article is used before the first adjective:

The sturdy and well-made car withstood the beating it took on the backwoods roads. (one car)

An article is used before an adjective modifying a noun which is implied but left unexpressed:

The exhibit featured *an* old and *a* new model.   (two models)

When two nouns joined by *and* are preceded by separate articles, then two separate persons or things are being denoted:

A secretary and *a* treasurer are needed in this company.

When two nouns joined by *and* are preceded by only one article, then only one person or thing is being denoted:

A secretary and treasurer is needed in this company.

When two things are so closely associated that they are considered to be a unit, only one article is used:

We have ordered *a* mortar and pestle.

PUNCTUATION WITH ADJECTIVES

A *compound adjective* is made up of two or more words combined to form a single modifying unit. Compound adjectives are hyphenated unless the first word ends in *ly:*

a red-headed man, a heart-to-heart talk, a ten-foot pole

a deep-seated bias, a pillar-to-post existence

But: a deeply appreciated gift, a cleverly worded note
a newly designed suit, a warmly felt answer

After a verb or linking verb, most compound adjectives drop their hyphenation so that the words originally combined regain their original force:

They talked *heart to heart.*

The feather was *bluish green.*

The speaker was *well known.*

Compound numbers are hyphenated; fractions are hyphenated only when they are used as adjectives:

There are *twenty-three* people in the class at present.

Twenty-three of us will go.

He bought the equipment at a *one-third* reduction in price.

          S   LV CA
But: *One third* of the money is mine.

Co-ordinate adjectives are adjectives which modify the same noun directly; they are set off by commas:

The *stiff, uncomfortable* chair hurt my back.

In this example the comma has the effect of *and.* Notice that the adjectives could also be reversed:

The *stiff* and *uncomfortable* chair hurt my back.

The *uncomfortable, stiff* chair hurt my back.

Their government was undermined by *cruel, unrelenting* economic forces.

Their government was undermined by *cruel* and *unrelenting* economic forces.

Their government was undermined by *unrelenting, cruel* economic forces.

Mr McGrath is a *sensible, patient, determined* man.

Mr. McGrath is a *sensible* and *patient* and *determined* man.

Mr. McGrath is a *patient, determined, sensible* man.

Complete Work Projects 20-22

WORK PROJECT 19

Using Adjectives and the
Degrees of Adjectives

A.   Underline each adjective and draw an arrow from it to the noun or pronoun it modifies.
Do not bother to underline articles.

Ex: The soap is *his*.   *Martha's old* Buick is *roomy*.

1.   The four boys asked six girls to attend the Thanksgiving dance.

2.   Sylvia's handkerchief was red and white.

3.   An article worthy of mention was published in this issue of that magazine.

4.   These telegrams have accumulated in the last four hours.

5.   A Polish dish was the main course at Bertha's dinner party.

6.   Her answer revealed her pessimistic outlook.

7.   A cane two inches longer will be satisfactory.

8.   Five bright copper pennies shimmered in the clear water.

9.   Mr. Hopkins' wife accepted the list price for our television set.

10.   Fewer people appeared on opening night.

B.   In the space provided, insert *a* or *an* to complete the sentence correctly.

1.   .... honorable man always considers his integrity first.

2.   Only .... union member could have dissuaded him.

3.   Better crust is obtained when .... egg is used.

4.   The pollsters described him as .... regular user of our product.

5.   He was .... historian from the old school.

6.   She spent .... hour with him yesterday.

7.   There is a good deal of difference between an apple and .... quince.

8.   It was a pleasure and .... honor to serve you.

9.   .... university is simply a collection of good minds.

10.   Now I am under .... obligation to Marie.

C. Choose the correct form in parentheses and write it down in the space at the right.

1. Mr. Thornton was the (more, most) energetic of the two men. ....

2. Harold received (more unanimous, most unanimous, more nearly unanimous, most nearly unanimous) approval than Russell. ....

3. Mr. Jones was the (more, most) optimistic member of the family. ....

4. My ring is (more perfect, more nearly perfect, perfecter) than yours. ....

5. Of the two winners, Charles is the (more, most) deserving. ....

6. Milton turned off onto the (narrowest, narrower, more narrow, most narrow) road in the county. ....

7. Of all the men here, he is the (more, most) productive. ....

8. He is the (less, least) sympathetic funeral director I have met. ....

9. The winning design was the (more, most, more nearly, most nearly) unique one submitted in the class. ....

10. Allen is the (better, best) player of the twins. ....

11. Have you seen a copy of Merdon's (latter, later) book? ....

12. (Less, Fewer) men have been laid off this spring. ....

13. Is he the (oldest, eldest) of the sons? ....

14. I refuse to carry the load one step (further, farther) down the road. ....

15. We must try to schedule (less, fewer) hours on the night shift. ....

16. Jean is taller than (any, any other) girl in the chorus. ....

17. Who could be (competenter, more competent) than Miss Badger? ....

18. She turns out more work than (anyone, anyone else) there. ....

19. The actress proved to be (lovelier, more lovelier) than I had remembered. ....

20. Marsha and her sister are of similar build, but I believe that Marsha is the (taller, tallest). ....

21. Jim dances in a (more graceful, gracefuller) way than his younger brother. ....

22. The final chapter of his book was the (less, least) interesting of all. ....

WORK PROJECT 20

Using Adjectives Correctly

A. Insert the correct form in the space provided at the right.

1. We had almost forgotten (them, those) display samples.　　1 ....

2. Mr. Unger followed a strict but (healthy, healthful) diet prescribed by his wife.　　2 ....

3. We traded the Ford for (that, that there) sports car.　　3 ....

4. Muriel and Phyllis agreed to become babysitters for (each other, one another).　　4 ....

5. The (three last, last three) sentences of his letter were full of remorse for what he had done.　　5 ....

6. (Those, That) kind of salesmen usually irritates me.　　6 ....

7. (This, These) type of appliances used to be popular.　　7 ....

8. John, Harry, Bart, and I corresponded with (each other, one another) all during the war.　　8 ....

9. These (two last, last two) analyses have been submitted by a reliable government official.　　9 ....

10. The two of them frequently passed (one another, each other) as they sprinted toward the finish line.　　10 ....

B. Many of the sentences listed below contain errors in the use of articles or other adjectives. Strike out unnecessary words or words incorrectly placed; insert new words where necessary. If a sentence is correct, place a C in the space at the right.

1. A husky and a belligerent-looking foreman stood there clenching his fists.　　1 ....

2. I only became acquainted with him last weekend.　　2 ....

3. A lawyer and tax consultant was lent us by the home office.　　3 ....

4. The actor and the director, Mr. Burns, accompanied us when we went backstage.　　4 ....

5. Both the green and blue stamps are redeemable here.　　5 ....

6. A truck and a trailer was parked beside the warehouse.   6 ....

7. As the secretary and the treasurer, it was Mr. Penn's obligation to endorse that check.   7 ....

8. Ingrid left a cotton and dacron coat lying on her seat, and now she can't find it.   8 ....

9. The present and former director of the club met yesterday in the employees' cafeteria.   9 ....

10. The child was only given money, not love.   10 ....

C. Insert hyphens or commas wherever they are required. Not all items will require punctuation.

1. every able bodied man

2. money making ability

3. part time jobs

4. a mid January clearance sale

5. half willing partners

6. closely guarded secrets

7. a door to door sales approach

8. a temporarily postponed meeting

9. three scantily clad models

10. low cost items

11. Mr. Cousins, the editor, is well known.

12. Mr. Spellman dislikes high pressure salesmanship.

13. The ten inch length of the one way ticket amused him.

14. One half the amount will be due in thirty days.

15. The fragrant penetrating aroma of the partially brewed coffee revived the red headed man.

16. Twenty one huge neon signs will be placed along the road at strategic well chosen places.

17. An all aluminum chair makes a pleasing useful addition to a well planned patio.

18. The Mastersons were content with second class accommodations.

19. His observations were up to date in every respect.

20. A questioning half suspicious expression came to the face of the recently adopted child.

21. She was an attractive friendly skillful interviewer.

22. Thirty six dollars is not a large down payment.

23. More than one fourth of the members were absent.

24. Mr. Samson was ably defended by his quick witted lawyers.

25. A grayish green rug would counteract the severity of the other furnishings.

26. The visits were well timed.

27. Mr. Smithers was offended by her holier than thou attitude.

28. The cleverly worded sentiment on the card pleased him.

29. Only six foot boards were used in the fence.

30. The three apprentices have been well trained.

WORK PROJECT 21

Using the Comparative and Superlative Degrees of Adjectives

A.   Fill in the blanks with the correct form of the adjective in parentheses or with the answer called for.

1.   Of the two plans proposed, I think the one which Mr. Jones has outlined is the ....   (*good*)

2.   His cold is much .... this morning.   (*bad*)

3.   That crime was the .... of the two he committed.   (*bad*)

4.   I have looked up the distances to both towns, and I find that Wheeling is the ....   (*far*)

5.   If you want the .... of these two pupils to do the work, choose William.   (*good*)

6.   Chicago is the .... of the two cities.   (*near*)

7.   Both shipments were received in bad condition, but the first one was by far the ....   (*bad*)

8.   Mr. Smith has been the .... of the two executives. (*competent*)

9.   John is .... than any .... boy in the class. (*studious*)

10.   When two objects are compared, use the .... degree of the adjective.

11.   The comparative degree of the adjective *merry* is ....

12.   The climate there is .... than in any .... part of the country.   (*dry*)

B.   Fill in with the correct form (this, these; that, those).

13.   Please bring me .... papers on the table in the dining room.

14.   You should get a good deal out of .... study of adjectives.

15.   .... kinds of oranges grow well in California.

16.   She always prefers .... kind of grapes.

17.   I have often used .... kind of machines.

18.   As I look at them, I don't believe .... data are correct.

Fill in the correct adjectives:

.... kind of libraries   .... species (singular)
.... analyses   .... memoranda
.... kinds of sentences   .... type of cars

C.   Compose sentences for the following items.

Ex: worse His rating was worse than mine. ....

1.   fewer ....

2.   the most promising ....

3.   less attentive ....

4.   the least tiring ....

5.   more nearly perfect ....

6.   more tactful ....

7.   friendliest ....

8.   less ....

WORK PROJECT 22

Correcting Copy

The following letter contains many errors in the use of adjectives. Place a check mark (√) after the number of each line that contains one or more errors.

12-A Larkin Lane

Purdy, California

April 29, 19—

Mr. Anton A. Kerper, Vice President

Southern Pacific Railroad

10 Market Street

San Franciso 11, California

Dear Mr. Kerper:

Your advertisement for a male secretary seemed very	1 ....
attractive to me, especially since I enjoy traveling and prefer	2 ....
doing work that is different and challenging. Your requirement	3 ....
and my ability were made for one another. Please consider me as	4 ....
an applicant for the position.	5 ....
I am twenty three years of age and have no immediate plans	6 ....
for marrying. My two first jobs were basically secretarial. I	7 ....
worked as assistant to a lumber mill foreman for one summer after	8 ....
graduating from high school, and I worked part-time as night clerk	9 ....
at a travel agency in San Diego while I completed my junior	10 ....
college education. Since being released from the U. S. Navy, I	11 ....
have been employed as the secretary and treasurer of the Purdy	12 ....
Cooperative Store in Purdy. Though it is a pleasant prosperous	13 ....
town, Purdy offers me less chances of advancement than any place	14 ....
in the state.	15 ....

Letters confirming my character, ability, and experience   16 ....

can be obtained from Mr. A. L. Potter, Potter Travel Agency,   17 ....

401 Bay Street, San Diego; Mr. T. W. Arenson, Purdy Cooperative   18 ....

Store, Purdy California; and Lieutenant Commander C. C. Smith,   19 ....

87 Oak Knoll, Denver, Colorado. The latter was my immediate   20 ....

superior while I was a court reporter in the Navy.   21 ....

It is important for you to hire someone who will accept the   22 ....

conditions of employment you have mentioned. I assure you that I   23 ....

can adjust to those conditions. Occasional stints of long, un-   24 ....

interrupted work and pressure from last minute changes are healthy   25 ....

for a man. I feel able to survive those type of demands.   26 ....

If you are interested in my application, I will be glad to   27 ....

come to San Francisco so that you can inquire farther into my   28 ....

qualifications.   29 ....

Yours very truly,

Nathaniel Boswell

Nathaniel Boswell

In the spaces provided below, first list the number of the line which contains error(s). Then supply the correction(s) in the other spaces. If a hyphen or comma is needed, be sure to include the words affected.

Ex: ....4....   ....each other............   ....

....

....

....

....

....

....

....

....

....

9 ADVERBS

Adverbs involve less likelihood of mistakes in writing than adjectives, yet it is important to learn to control them so that they correctly modify verbs, adjectives, or other adverbs. Because they, too, are modifying words, adverbs are often confused with adjectives in form and function. Furthermore, adverbs have a great deal of flexibility in their position in a sentence; they "hop around" more than other one-word parts of speech. Aside from *no one* and *no* and *nobody*, adverbs are the chief words used to express negative ideas: *not, scarcely, never,* etc. Using two such words in one main thought is a violation of a widely observed convention.

IDENTIFYING ADVERBS

An adverb modifies or limits the meaning of

a **verb**	Mr. Carney worked *quietly*.
an **adjective**	. . . a *very* efficient worker.
an **adverb**	The cards were printed *exceptionally* well.

An adverb answers many questions, but the pertinent ones in dealing with one-word parts of speech are these:

How?	I spoke *fast*. The machine ran *smoothly*.
When?	The conference ended *yesterday*. Can you leave *now*?
Where?	The people went *home*. Serge put his coat *there*.
To what degree?	Their response was *very* unusual. Anson walked *really* fast.

Normally adverbs are formed by adding *ly* to adjective forms:

Adjective	The performance was *satisfactory*.
Adverb	The entertainers performed *satisfactorily*.
Adjective	James seemed *calm*.
Adverb	He behaved *calmly* in the emergency.

A handful of important adverbs do not end in *ly*. They are easily remembered because they are so commonly used: *almost, always, ever, fast, here, never, now, often, only, seldom, sometime, soon, then, there, today, tomorrow, too, very, yesterday, not*.

An adverb is the most flexible part of speech. It can occur in many sentence positions. When it modifies an adjective or another adverb, it usually occurs *before* the word being modified (*annoyingly* shy, *too* boldly). When it modifies a verb, however, an adverb can occur almost anywhere in a sentence. It may occur before the verb, after the verb, or even between a helping word and the main verb; it may begin or end the sentence. Notice how many positions the word *soon* can occupy:

> *Soon* this project will require additional personnel.
>
> This project *soon* will require additional personnel.
>
> This project will *soon* require additional personnel.
>
> This project will require additional personnel *soon*.

THE DEGREES OF ADVERBS

The following sentences illustrate the different degrees of the adverb *fluently:*

> Mr. Millrod speaks *fluently*.
>
> Mr. Millrod speaks *more fluently* than Mr. Collings.
>
> Mr. Millrod speaks the *most fluently* of all the executives.

The degrees of adverbs are formed in the following ways:

	POSITIVE	COMPARATIVE	SUPERLATIVE
WORDS OF	late	later	latest
ONE SYLLABLE:	soon	sooner	soonest
	fast	faster	fastest
ADVERBS	quickly	more quickly	most quickly
ENDING IN *ly*:	acidly	more acidly	most acidly
	gracefully	more gracefully	most gracefully

The words *less* and *least* are used with an adverb to show lower degree:

> This particular Frenchman did not argue *energetically*.
> He argued *less energetically* than the other one.
> He argued the *least energetically* of all.

A few commonly used adverbs have irregular comparative and superlative degrees:

POSITIVE	COMPARATIVE	SUPERLATIVE
badly	worse	worst
far	farther	farthest
	further	furthest
much	more	most
well	better	best

SPECIAL PROBLEMS IN USING ADVERBS

Avoiding Double Negatives

Though in some other languages it is possible to use many negative words to establish the intensity of an idea, in English we don't appreciate two negative words in the same thought:

Double negative	She *didn't hardly* finish in time.
	They *couldn't barely* determine the difference.
Correct	She *hardly* finished in time.
	They *could barely* determine the difference.

Placing *only* and *also*

Only and *also* acquire quite different meanings, depending on their sentence positions. Be sure to insert them where they relate most precisely to the word being modified:

> *Only* the threat deterred him.
>
> The threat *only* deterred him.
>
> The threat deterred *only* him.
>
> We *also* spoke in favor of the petition.
>
> We signed the petition, *also*.   (also-too)

Farther; further

Farther is preferred for reference to distance; *further,* for reference to time, quantity, or degree:

> His journey took him *farther* than John's.
>
> He pursued the point *further* than was necessary.

Sometime; some time

Sometime is used as an adverb meaning at one time or another in the future or at some unspecified time. The phrase *some time* consists of an *adjective* and *noun:*

> *Sometime* I will take you with me.
>
> *Some time* will be required to straighten out this mess.

Confusion of Adjectives and Adverbs

A very common error is to use an adjective instead of an adverb to modify a verb, adjective, or adverb:

> The ball was thrown back to the pitcher *quick*.   (*quickly*)
>
> She always wears *real* attractive clothes.   (*really* or *very*)
>
> The racing car swerved *real* crazily.   (*really* or *very*)

After linking verbs, be sure to use an adjective:

The roses smell *fragrant*.	**Avoid:**	The roses smell ~~*fragrantly*~~.
They felt *bad*.		They felt ~~*badly*~~.
The music sounds *good*.		The music sounds ~~*well*~~.

Most; almost

Most is an adjective when it occurs before a noun; *almost* is an adverb used in front of an adjective:

> *Most* customers appreciate courtesy.
>
> *Almost* all our customers appreciate courtesy.
>
> **Avoid:**   ~~*Most*~~ all customers appreciate courtesy.

Good; well

Good is always an adjective; *well* can be used as an adjective to mean *in good health,* but more commonly it is used as an adverb:

My minister told me that I was *good.*

My doctor told me that I was *well.*

As a tennis player, I am not *good.*

I do not play tennis *well.*

I have not been *well* for the past month.

He performed *well* in spite of the difficulties.

The family remained *well* during the rest of the winter.

Avoid: I do not play tennis ~~good~~.

He performed ~~good~~ in spite of the difficulties.

Complete Work Projects 23 and 24

WORK PROJECT 23

Using Adverbs Correctly

A. Draw an arrow from each adverb to the word it modifies. If an adverb appears to modify a whole statement, then draw the arrow to the verb.

1. The dog barked wildly yesterday.

2. Seldom does the paper make a very serious mistake.

3. She always sings only one song.

4. Almost all colors are available now.

5. Today we will test the materials critically before we send them there.

6. Soon the crowd will be roaring ecstatically.

7. Mrs. Worthy spoke rapidly and gestured frequently.

8. This coffee is not too hot.

9. My husband often drives fast, but I never do.

10. If the children are unusually bright, they should never be held here beyond one term.

B. Fill in the space at the right with the correct form of the adverb in parentheses.

1. Helen transcribes her notes the (well) of the two girls.   ....

2. Of all the men in the barracks, Tom spoke (scornfully).   ....

3. Bronson dressed (lower degree of stylishly) than his younger brother.   ....

4. He arrived (soon) of all.   ....

5. Miss Dawes complained (bitterly) than anyone else in class.   ....

C. Insert the adverb in parentheses in the most effective position.

Ex: I sold ∧ ten tickets for the benefit performance.   *(only)*

1. They were in need of medical supplies.   *(critically)*

2. One other man protested the measure. (*only* to relate to *man*)

3. I left a note with Mr. Tenery. (*also* to mean an additional action)

4. The outlets were promised for one week. (*only* to mean not more than one week)

5. He wrote down my name and address. (*only* to mean not more than one action)

D. Choose the correct form in parentheses and write the answer in the space at the right.

1. The office boy comes around (regular, regularly) at four o'clock.

2. (Almost, Most) every letter has been addressed in longhand.

3. He (didn't hardly care, hardly cared) about his responsibility.

4. Bertram and I were (very, real) disturbed by the delay.

5. The husband hiked much (farther, further) than his wife.

6. We must go there (some time, sometime).

7. The lecturer extended the discussion (farther, further) than was wise.

8. The problem was solved (different, differently) from what I had anticipated.

9. We (couldn't barely, could barely) fill the last two orders.

10. (Most, Almost) all the candy machines are being overhauled.

11. We left her there, and we felt (bad, badly) about losing her.

12. Gelatin can have a (real, really) fine flavor in desserts.

13. The markings look (faint, faintly) at a distance.

14. Within a week Jack was walking as (good, well) as ever.

15. That game must (sure, surely) have been a close one!

16. The postponement was (real, very) disappointing.

17. Miss Briggs traced the call more quickly than (most, almost) any other operator could have done.

18. Mitchell (shouldn't, shouldn't never) return the soiled goods to the stockroom.

19. She looked (bad, badly) after her recent illness.

20. We three have (sure, surely) deserved the reward more than you think.

WORK PROJECT 24

Correcting Copy

The following letter contains many errors in the use of adverbs. Place a check mark (√) after the number of each line that contains one or more errors.

WESTERN PAINT & CHEMICAL CO.

1040 Vallejo   Phoenix, Arizona

October 11, 19—

Mr. A. K. Arthur, Manager

Paul Smith Company

One Armory Street

Long Beach, California

Dear Mr. Arthur:

As we wrote you earlier, we are using Filcheck units on most	1 ....
all our production lines. The units are working good with one	2 ....
small exception. The significant variance in pigment level in	3 ....
the bottles from our local supplier causes frequent adjustment to	4 ....
the light intensity.	5 ....
The detection of low-level bottles has been improved con-	6 ....
siderable. We originally observed that the lack of inspection by	7 ....
a checker using transmitted light decreased our pickup of bottles	8 ....
with pin holes, open-handle seams, and windows in the body of the	9 ....
bottles. When transmitted light was not used, the checker wasn't	10 ....
hardly able to see the high fills which are caused by pin holes	11 ....
and defective seams. Now, by using transmitted light, we find	12 ....
that detecting low-level bottles is the less of our problems.	13 ....
We anticipate inconveniencing you no farther.	14 ....

We bring this situation to your attention because you may   15 ....

experience trouble in your warehouse and in the retail trade   16 ....

from these low-level bottles. Sometime may be required to   17 ....

locate and recall what we have already sent out. We have   18 ....

advised Allstate Can Company of these problems. They are real   19 ....

sorry for the inconvenience to us and are doing their best to   20 ....

minimize defects.   21 ....

Sincerely yours,

WESTERN PAINT & CHEMICAL CO.

CCdeVries

C. C. de Vries
Vice President

CCdeV:ty

In the spaces provided below, first list the number of the line which contains error(s). Then supply the correction(s) in the other spaces.

Ex: ...1...   ....almost................   ....

       ....

       ....

       ....

       ....

       ....

       ....

       ....

       ....

       ....

10 PREPOSITIONS

A preposition is a word or unit of several words that takes a noun or pronoun as its object and shows a relationship between the object and some other word in the sentence:

The conferences *with the union spokesman* continued *for a week*.

This relationship can be described grammatically as either adjectival or adverbial:

The office for the executive will be completed on time.

The main reason for studying prepositions is to learn how effective they can be as joining words which establish logical connections between one part of a sentence and another part. They make it possible to expand a sentence thought by adding to it smaller grammatical units which would otherwise require separate sentences:

A reward was offered for the lost gun. | The owner *of the lost gun* offered a reward.
The owner offered the reward.

IDENTIFYING PREPOSITIONS

A preposition is never incorporated into a sentence by itself; it must always introduce a prepositional phrase, a group of words beginning with a preposition and ending with a noun or pronoun:

The compromise *on the plans* was approved *by the membership*.

When you speak or read aloud, you normally inflect a prepositional phrase as though it were one thought-unit:

The compromise│on the plans│was approved│by the membership.

What you have thus perceived is that a prepositional phrase functions as a single word. Grammatically a prepositional phrase serves as either an adjective or an adverb:

Adjective   The change *in the schedule* presented a problem *in logistics.* (*In the schedule* and *in logistics* are adjectives answering the question *What kind?*)

The itinerary *for your trip* has been modified.
(*For your trip* is an adjective answering the question *Which one?*)

Adverb   The plane will leave *at ten o'clock.*
(*At ten o'clock* answers the adverb question *When?*)

The agreement was made *with your knowledge.*
(*With your knowledge* answers the adverb question *How?*)

If only we could look *into the future!*
(*Into the future* answers the adverb question *Where?*)

The performance was cancelled *because of her illness.*
(*Because of her illness* answers the adverb question *Why?*)

Like adjectives and adverbs, prepositional phrases occur in well-defined positions. A prepositional phrase used as an adjective follows the noun it modifies:

The campaign for the governorship was handled wisely.

A ship without a full cargo means a loss of profit.

The retiring vice-president received a box of cigars.

Prepositional phrases used as adverbs frequently occur at the beginning or end of a sentence pattern, or after the verb, but they can never occur immediately before the verbs they modify:

By January the reorganization will have been effected.

The reorganization will have been effected by January.

The buyers have agreed on a policy.

Notice the awkwardness that would result in putting the adverb phrase before the noun it modifies:

The reorganization by January will have been effected.

The buyers on a policy have agreed.

When a prepositional phrase occurs after the object in a S-V-O pattern, common sense is the key to determining what is being modified:

ADJ.
Mr. Janus criticized the article in the journal.

Common sense is also the key to determining the function of prepositional phrases that occur in sequence:

ADV.   **ADJ.**
That letter was filed in the cabinet near the door.

ADV.   **ADV.**
We sent the samples to you in a large envelope.

ELIMINATING ERRORS IN USING PREPOSITIONAL PHRASES

At, To

At is used to indicate a position attained, sought, or concerned; *to* is used to indicate a motion or direction toward somthing:

> They were *at* the meeting last week.
>
> They walked *to* the meeting with friends.
>
> **Avoid:**   They were *to* the meeting last week.

Between, Among

Use *between* with two objects; *among,* with three or more:

> The referee stepped *between* the two fighters.
>
> The presents were divided *among* the members of the family.
>
> **Avoid:**   The presents were divided *between* the members of the family.

Beside, Besides

Use *beside* to mean *next to;* use *besides* to mean *in addition to:*

> Come sit *beside* me.
>
> Is anyone at home *besides* you?
>
> **Avoid:**   Is anyone at home *beside* you?   (Unless you mean just that!)

In, Into

Use *in* to indicate action or state of being within a certain place; use *into* to indicate motion from one place to another place:

> The coach stormed *into* the locker room.
>
> He shouted angrily *in* the locker room.
>
> **Avoid:**   The injured player was carried *in* the locker room.

Of

Of should not be used in the following combinations:

> We got the information *off* (*off of*) her.
>   Better: We got the information *from* her.
>
> They looked *inside of* (*outside of*) the house.
>   Better: They looked *inside* (*outside*) the house.
>
> The apple fell *off of* the shelf.
>   Better: The apple fell *off* the shelf.
>
> I should *of* known better.   (a careless pronunciation of *have*)
>   Correct: I should *have* known better.
>
> All *of* the men were ready.
> Both *of* the girls seemed reluctant.
>   Better: All the men were ready.
>   Both the girls seemed reluctant.

Note.   *All of* and *both of* are correctly used only when followed by pronouns:

> *All of them* were absent.
> *Both of us* can go.

To

Do not confuse *to, too,* and *two:*

> She brought the broth *to* Grandmother.   *(preposition)*
> She sold *two* tickets.   *(adjective)*
> She was *too* optimistic about her chances.   *(adverb of degree)*
> She, *too,* has become optimistic.   (with the meaning of *also*)

PREPOSITIONS USED IDIOMATICALLY

Many prepositions have acquired fixed, conventional uses in combinations with other words, especially verbs. Some of the most important combinations are listed below. An unabridged dictionary like *Webster's 3rd Ed.* is the best reference for checking idiomatic combinations ending in a preposition.

Accompanied by (a person)	She was accompanied *by* her mother.
Accompanied with (an object)	The request was accompanied *with* a check.
Agree to (accept terms)	I agree *to* your conditions without reservation.
Agree with (an opinion)	Do you agree *with* me about the economy?
Agree on (*upon*) (a plan)	If they can agree *upon* a plan, the two men will become partners.
Agree in (principle)	He at least agreed *in* principle with what you suggested.
Angry with (a person)	Are you still angry *with* the shopforeman?
Angry at (an object or situation)	She was angered *at* the long delay.
Buy from (avoid *of*)	Whom did you buy these tools *from?*
Compare to (things of unlike class)	Freud compared the conscious mind *to* the tip of a protruding iceberg.
Compare with (things of like class)	It is easy to compare your debts *with* mine.
Concur in (an opinion)	Miss Hodges won't concur *in* that opinion.
Concur with (a person)	He concurred *with* me in knocking out the east wall of the delivery room.
Convenient for (a purpose)	The balcony is convenient *for* a view of the city.
Convenient to (a person or object)	The grocery store is convenient *to* your apartment.
Differ with (an opinion)	I differ *with* you.
Differ from (in quality)	The workmanship differs *from* what I had expected.
Different from (not *than*)	This new model is different *from* all the others.
Differently from (not *than*)	He behaved differently *from* the other men.
Deal in (merchandise)	We deal *in* used cars of foreign make.
Deal with (a subject)	How can we deal *with* a price war?
Enter on, upon, in (the record)	They wished it entered *on* the record that they had turned themselves in.
Enter into (an agreement)	Wilson and Sons has entered *into* a long-term contract with our firm.

Independent of (not *from*)   He always tried to be independent *of* his father.

Initiate into (not *in*)   I was initiated *into* the self-conscious rites of the junior executive.

OMITTING AND INSERTING PREPOSITIONS

Do not omit necessary prepositions:

Incorrect: He had no knowledge or respect *for* our traditions.
Correct: He had no knowledge *of* or respect *for* our traditions.
Preferred: He had no knowledge *of* our traditions or respect *for* them.

Omit unnecessary prepositions:

Incorrect: Where are you visiting *at?*
Correct: Where are you visiting?

Incorrect: I can't help *from* complaining again.
Correct: I can't help complaining again.

Incorrect: Where is he going *to?*
Correct: Where is he going?

COMMON PREPOSITIONS

above	above the poster
after	after the inquiry
along	along the rafters
around	around the land
behind	behind the desk
beneath	beneath the tree
beyond	beyond the hills
but (except)	all but one
down	down the pipe
during	during the fall sales
except	except him
for	for the weekend
in	in the group
like	like a fool
near	near you
of	of the majority
off	off the truck
on	on the freeway
outside	outside the fence
over	over the area
since	since last May
through	through the report
to	to the store
toward	toward greater remuneration
under	under control
until	until dawn
up	up the creek
with	with your approval
without	without her consent

according to	according to the rumor
because of	because of the fire
as far as	as far as the golf course
in front of	in front of the building
in reference to	in reference to your comment
in regard to	in regard to your question
instead of	instead of a check

Complete Work Project 25

WORK PROJECT 25

Using Prepositions

A. Underline each prepositional phrase and draw an arrow from it to the word it modifies. If a phrase seems to modify the whole sentence, draw the arrow to the verb. In the space at the right, state whether the phrase is functioning as an adjective or adverb.

1. A pile of bills arrived in the morning mail. ....

2. Two plumbers sauntered into the kitchen of the cafe. ....

3. The signature on this letter was made in red ink. ....

4. Before the performance the director gathered the cast for a pep talk. ....

5. The land near the lake was purchased by a speculator. ....

6. An apprentice built the model for the boat in his spare time. ....

7. With your permission he can remain here until Tuesday. ....

8. Miss Cox had not anticipated such a demand for our products. ....

9. He walked down the street in a great hurry. ....

10. Within an hour the notices had been distributed to everyone. ....

B. Write the correct preposition in the space at the right.

1. The gratuity was divided equally (among, between) the three waitresses. ....

2. Jim was (at, to) the last business meeting. ....

3. Have we overlooked anyone (beside, besides) him? ....

4. Should we enter (in, into) an agreement with them? ....

5. We can file only ten papers (in, into) each folder. ....

6. The old furniture was moved (in, into) the storage room. ....

7. The work was shared (among, between) us two. ....

8. I borrowed some carbon paper (from, off of) her. ....

9. (Inside, Inside of) the house it was very comfortable. ....

10. You are (to, two, too) eager to succeed. ....

11. (All, All of) the papers were ready. ....

12. (Both, Both of) them would benefit from the change. ....

13. I took those (off, off of) the shelf. ....

14. Both of them should (have, of) known better. ....

15. (Both, Both of) our employees are friendly. ....

C. Fill in the correct preposition in the space at the right.

1. Have you been initiated (in, into) your father's club? ....

2. Do you agree (to, with) the terms of sale? ....

3. Is that hotel convenient (to, for) holding the spring conference? ....

4. I know how to deal (in, with) matters like those. ....

5. He always reacts differently (than, from) his brother. ....

6. Richard cannot agree (with, to) our opinion. ....

7. Tomorrow we will enter (on, into) a new agreement. ....

8. It won't be long until they are independent (of, from) us. ....

9. The poet compared her eyes (to, with) pools of water. ....

10. We buy these things (of, from) independent jobbers. ....

11. Do you concur (in, with) that opinion? ....

12. Are you angry (at, with) me? ....

13. If she ever concurs (with, in) me, I'll be surprised. ....

14. He differs (with, from) everyone else on the matter of speeding up deliveries. ....

15. His figures are different (than, from) yours. ....

16. Do you deal (with, in) stocks and bonds? ....

17. The new shopping center is convenient (to, for) our weekly conference. ....

18. Their woolens didn't compare favorably (to, with) ours. ....

19. How can the machine be so different (than, from) the illustration? ....

20. I was angry (at, with) the old car. ....

D. Cross out any unnecessary prepositions and insert any necessary ones.

1. He took that book off of my desk.

2. Where is the last survey filed at?

3. Mr. Quan had great respect and devotion to his duty.

4. What use is this syllabus without an index?

5. Miss Larsen can't help from liking Mr. Boone.

6. Where are they going to?

7. Both of the employers insist on college graduates.

8. Mr. Burgess denied interest or responsibility for the change.

9. All of the factors were considered before a decision was reached.

10. I waited for her outside of the building.

E. If the italicized phrase is correctly and effectively placed, put a C in the space at the right. If it is incorrectly or ineffectively placed, in the space at the right put down the word after which the phrase should be placed. If the phrase should begin the sentence, write down the first word of the phrase and capitalize it.

1. *As the treasurer* you should see to it that the work is finished. ....

2. The office has been remodeled *for the new president.* ....

3. Your account leaves the proposed site of the new building *out of mention.* ....

4. This company has been retiring its senior members at half pay for *eighteen years.* ....

5. We can reinvest the money immediately *with these profits.* ....

6. An interest rate will be allowed on that investment of *of three per cent.* ....

7. May we quote *to you* the summary of our last financial statement? ....

8. The compliment was appreciated *on the arrangement for the banquet.* ....

9. Our listing of furniture will be mailed to you *for reception rooms.* ....

10. No one gave us the information which we need *but him.* ....

F. Supply the correct preposition in the following idiomatic combinations. Use a dictionary when you are uncertain. A few combinations will permit the use of several different prepositions; however, you will be given credit for supplying just one correct preposition.

1. to agree .... the transaction

2. to participate .... the contest

3. to be acquainted .... the facts of the case

4. to look .... your letter

5. to be accompanied .... his secretary

6. to reconcile his action .... his decision

7. to distinguish .... the two colors

8. to comply .... the regulations

9. to attend .... a business

10. to agree .... ourselves

11. to be happy .... the outcome

12. to choose .... the three of them

13. to differ .... public opinion

14. to disagree .... the opposition

15. to be capable .... superior work

16. to abstain .... writing the complaint

17. to adhere .... a fixed idea

18. to account .... a decision

19. to be different .... an object

20. to be disappointed .... a person

21. to absolve .... blame

22. to be delighted .... a circumstance

23. to inquire .... a person

24. to be angry .... things

25. to be angry .... persons

26. to be employed .... a salary of

27. to depend .... a person

28. to confide .... a person

29. to deal .... problems

30. to concur .... a person

31. to be conversant .... the entire matter

32. to agree .... a person

33. to be different .... the other

34. in contrast .... the others

35. a taste .... art

36. to be accessory .... the crime

37. to confer .... a lawyer

38. to be identical .... the others

39. to accede .... his request

40. to take exception .... a statement

11 CONJUNCTIONS

A conjunction is a connecting word that joins words, phrases, and clauses. Together with prepositions, conjunctions make possible a great economy in writing. They make it possible to write about more than one person or object at a time, to assert two or more actions, and to express several modifying concepts. More importantly, they enable us to establish a logical relationship between a main idea and one of less importance. Without them there would be very little sophistication or stylistic variation in our expression.

COORDINATE CONJUNCTIONS

Coordinate conjunctions join constructions of equal weight or importance. There are six coordinate conjunctions: *and, or, nor, for, but,* and *yet.* All of them are illustrated below. Notice that in the third example two predicates are being joined.

1. Requisitions and receipts are kept in this drawer.

2. Did you sign your name on this line or on that one?

3. The tourist agency planned our itinerary and secured our passports.

4. Mr. O'Connell and Mr. Downs have accepted other positions, but Mr. Browning is still considering our offer.

5. The supervisor decided that the adjustment department had made the error and that the difference should be credited to the customer's account.

6. The new associate was not free to accept the appointment, for he was still handling the MacDonald contract.

7. Horace was overworked, yet he never complained about his burden.

Punctuation with Coordinate Conjunctions

Generally a comma is used before a coordinate conjunction when it joins two independent clauses. If the clauses are very short and closely related in meaning, the comma is often omitted. A comma is required before *for* (to prevent confusion with the preposition *for*) and recommended before *but* and *yet*.

> The Petersens did not attend the Culinary Arts Exhibit, nor did they publicize it locally.
>
> Mr. Morton hesitated about the price, for his wife frowned on extravagance.
> (Without the comma after *price*, the word *for* might be mistaken for a preposition, thus causing the reader unnecessary difficulty in grasping the correct meaning.)
>
> Shall I forward the goods to Springdale, or can you pick them up at our warehouse on Fremont Street?

When only two words or phrases or dependent clauses are joined by a coordinate conjunction, no comma is used:

> The *custodian* and the *charwoman* also submitted suggestions.
>
> New carpeting will be placed *in the reception room* and *in the lounge*.
>
> Mrs. Wagner decided *that the article was too long* and *that it required extensive editing*.

CORRELATIVE CONJUNCTIONS

There are several pairs of correlative conjunctions:

> *either . . . or   neither . . . nor   not only . . . but also   both . . . and   the more . . . the more*

Ex: *Neither* the paper angels *nor* the tinsel bells proved to be profitable items.

> The brochure included *not only* a picture of the island *but also* a description of its recreational advantages.
>
> *The more* desperate he became, *the more* he relied upon foolish excuses to justify his behavior.
>
> *Both* Richard *and* Paul inspected the shipment yesterday.

Use a comma with correlative conjunctions only when they join two independent clauses:

> *Either* the regional office will send you a notice, *or* Mr. Townsend will telephone you.
>
> *The more* I considered her remark, *the more* disturbed I became.

Complete Work Project 26

SUBORDINATE CONJUNCTIONS

A subordinate conjunction is used to introduce a dependent clause and join it to an independent clause. It joins a minor thought to a major thought. In the following illustrations, the dependent clause has been blocked and the subordinate conjunction set off by a slant line. Notice it is the subordinate conjunction which makes a clause dependent.

A telegram arrived ⌑while/you were in conference⌑.

The inspector asked ⌑where/we kept the fuel⌑.

The summary will be prepared ⌑before/the chairman needs it⌑.

⌑That/she was dissatisfied⌑ never occurred to me.

The most commonly used subordinate conjunctions are listed below. You should keep in mind, however, that some of these words can be used as other parts of speech, chiefly as prepositions. A subordinate conjunction must introduce a clause and make it dependent on an independent clause to complete its meaning.

after	on condition that	unless
although	provided	until
as	since	when
as soon as	so that	where
because	than	whether
before	that	while
if	though	
in order that	till	

RELATIVE PRONOUNS

Some dependent clauses are introduced by relative pronouns (*who, whom, whose, which, that, whatever, whichever, whoever, whomever*) that serve to relate a dependent clause to an independent clause. Often the relative pronoun serves as the subject or object of the dependent clause, or as the object of a verb in the dependent clause:

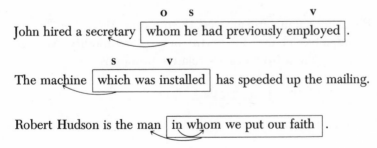

DEPENDENT CLAUSES AS PARTS OF SPEECH

Subordinate conjunctions and relative pronouns merit a good deal of attention, since they provide a means whereby minor thoughts are related to major thoughts. These logical relationships can be explained grammatically be saying that a dependent clause serves as a noun, an adjective, or an adverb. The following groups of sentences have been arranged to illustrate how clauses can function as parts of speech.

Noun Clauses

A noun clause is easily identified because it patterns as a noun. It serves as a subject, an object, a complement noun, or an object of a preposition. A noun clause is commonly introduced by *that,* but almost any other subordinate conjunction can be used to introduce a noun clause.

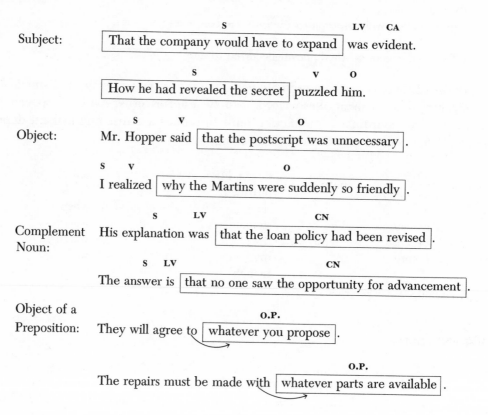

Subject: That the company would have to expand │ was evident.

How he had revealed the secret │ puzzled him.

Object: Mr. Hopper said │ that the postscript was unnecessary │.

I realized │ why the Martins were suddenly so friendly │.

Complement Noun: His explanation was │ that the loan policy had been revised │.

The answer is │ that no one saw the opportunity for advancement │.

Object of a Preposition: They will agree to │ whatever you propose │.

The repairs must be made with │ whatever parts are available │.

Adjective Clauses

An adjective clause describes a noun and answers the question *What kind?* or *Which one?* Like prepositional phrases, adjective clauses follow the nouns they modify. Adjective clauses are easily identified because they are introduced by relative pronouns.

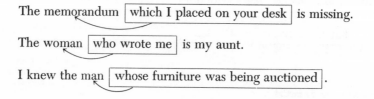

The memorandum │ which I placed on your desk │ is missing.

The woman │ who wrote me │ is my aunt.

I knew the man │ whose furniture was being auctioned │.

Adverb Clauses

An adverb answers the questions *How? Where? When?* and *To what degree?* Dependent clauses used as adverbs answer three additional questions: *Why? Under what condition?* and *With what concession?* Adverb clauses normally occur after an independent clause.

When?   I have not seen Mr. Potts since he returned from Mexico .

Where?   The file cabinets should be placed where they will be convenient .

How?   Mr. Hawkins hesitated as if he were reluctant to speak .

To what
degree?   We worked as hard as we could .

Why?   The policy was canceled because it was too expensive .

Under what
condition?   I can't go now unless I am properly relieved .

With what
concession?   Dorothy continued to speak, although she felt uncomfortable .

Note.   Frequently a subordinate conjunction or relative pronoun is implied but left out of a sentence:

He said (that) he could go.
The book (which) Ann wrote is still being used.

PUNCTUATION WITH DEPENDENT CLAUSES

Noun Clauses

Because they function as nouns, noun clauses are not set off by commas. A comma is never used to separate the parts of a basic sentence pattern; therefore, a noun clause should not be separated from the pattern it serves in. A comma is never used between a preposition and its object.

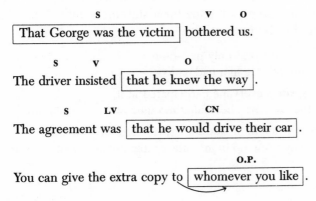

Adjective Clauses

Depending on whether or not they are required for the identification of the nouns they describe, adjective clauses are considered to be restrictive or nonrestrictive.

The woman *who returned the newspaper* works on the fourth floor.
(Restrictive: Which woman works on the fourth floor?)

Charlotte Green, *who returned the newspaper,* works on the fourth floor.
(Nonrestrictive: The adjective clause presents additional information not needed to identify which woman.)

Generally an adjective clause is nonrestrictive when it follows a proper noun, but notice the distinction made in the following sentences:

John Smith, *whom I interviewed last week,* was once a boxer.

The John Smith *whom I interviewed last week* was once a boxer.

In the second sentence the speaker is trying to specify which particular John Smith. Presumably there were at least two John Smiths under discussion.

Here are additional illustrations of restrictive and nonrestrictive clauses:

The man who built this house designed it himself.
Richard, who built this house, designed it himself.

I offered to buy the car which he had damaged.
I offered to buy the Ford, which he had damaged.
I offered to buy the Ford which he had damaged.   (more than one Ford involved)

Adverb Clauses

The terms *restrictive* and *nonrestrictive* also explain adverb clauses when they occur in their normal position following the main clause. If an adverb clause is nonrestrictive (if it could be omitted without changing the meaning of the main clause), it is set off.

Mr. Spoonbill was a concert pianist when he was younger.
(Mr. Spoonbill was a concert pianist only at a particular time of life; the adverb clause is therefore restrictive.)

Mr. Spoonbill was once a concert pianist, though you would never suspect it now.
(Here the adverb clause merely adds a further comment and could be left out of the sentence; it does not change the meaning of the main clause.)

Most adverb clauses are restrictive. Four adverb clauses are regularly nonrestrictive, those beginning with *a, though* and *although* and *b, since* and *as* when they mean *because.* When a clause beginning with *because* gives evidence for a statement rather than its cause, then that adverb clause is considered to be nonrestrictive.

Miss Carter is efficient, *though* she works only part-time.
We remained in our seats, *although* the film had ended.

The fund drive was a success, *since* everyone participated in it.
We abandoned the raft, *as* the river was becoming too narrow to navigate any longer.

They are bad boys, *because* my neighbor said so.   (evidence for statement)
They are bad boys *because* they grew up in an unfavorable environment.   (cause)

ERRORS IN USING CONJUNCTIONS

Provided, Providing

Both *provided* and *providing* are now acceptable as conjunctions, though *provided* is the conventionally preferred form.

Preferred: You can catch the plane *provided* you hurry.

Allowable: You can catch the plane *providing* you hurry.

As—As, So—As

In a positive comparison, use *as—as;* in a negative comparison, *so—as* is the conventionally preferred form, but *as—as* is also acceptable.

> He will be here *as* quickly *as* he can.
>
> She was not *so* friendly *as* her sister.
>
> (She was not *as* friendly *as* her sister.)

Incorrect Forms

Avoid these errors in using conjunctions:

> I cannot deny *that* (not *but* or *but that*) you are sincere.
>
> The shore line had no sooner become visible *than* (not *but*) the motor stopped.
>
> Please try *to* (not *and*) give us sufficient notice.
>
> Our new model is *longer,* but not so streamlined, as the old one.
>> (Correct: Our new model is *longer than* the old one but not so (as) streamlined.)

Like, As

It is preferable to use *like* as a preposition and *as* or *as if* as a conjunction, though some dictionaries now sanction the use of *like* as a conjunction.

> She makes enchiladas *as* her mother taught her.
>
> She looks *like* her mother.
>
> Acceptable but not preferred: She makes enchiladas *like* her mother taught her.

Except, Unless; Without, Unless

Except and *without* are prepositions and should not be used as conjunctions when *unless* is called for.

> No one was left in the building *except* me.
> Did they go *without* you?
>
> Incorrect: I won't leave ~~without~~ (*unless*) you leave, too.
>
> They will wait five minutes longer ~~except~~ (*unless*) you tell them otherwise.

Complete Work Project 27

WORK PROJECT 26

Identifying and Punctuating Coordinate Conjunctions

A. Underline the equal constructions which the conjunctions join. Indicate the conjunctions as in the example.

Ex: The horse jumped the fence and galloped across the field, but the cowboys did not chase him.

1. I knew that Cecilia would relinquish neither her position nor her authority.

2. Mr. Burton asked if the files were indexed and if the clerks were alert.

3. Nancy or Margaret can supply us with envelopes and stamps.

4. I have not had time to look at your figures or your conclusions, but I have forwarded your report to Mr. Bowes.

5. You conducted that interview with tact and skill.

6. Elaine asked how we posted the bills and how we routed them.

7. Miss Simpkins finished the work, for Miss Starch and Mrs. Parker were tabulating the daily receipts.

8. Fifty dollars seemed a large fine, but Wilbert paid it willingly.

9. Real and artificial fruits and flowers can be purchased at our new store.

10. Miss Harrold figured her income tax on the long form, for her deductions this year were larger than usual.

B. Put in the necessary commas.

1. Nell played and Roger sang.

2. The new duplicator and the old one are different for they operate on different principles.

3. One copy of your letter went to Alice and Ruby Garnett and another copy was sent to their father.

4. We do not wish to lose the contract yet we have already submitted our lowest bid.

5. Miss Lewis will issue the parking permits and Mr. Summers and Mr. Day will conduct the teachers on a tour of the plant.

6. We have never accurately predicted the volume of our Christmas business nor have our competitors.

7. William proofread all but ten of the galley proofs.

8. Mr. Snoddy bolted the door and sat down for an hour of private meditation.

9. Miss Curry will bring us some coffee and doughnuts or we can go next door for milk shakes and sandwiches.

10. The committee recommendations were submitted not only for your approval but also for your criticism.

11. He asked if the envelopes could be hand stamped for they contained color slides.

12. John Cotton assumed responsibility for all the animals but his brother protested.

13. You should repair this automobile or trade it in on a new one.

14. Additional fringe benefits were discussed at the March meeting of the stockholders and also at the September meeting of the employees' organization.

15. Our shipping season is nearly over but I am sure we can accommodate you.

16. Neither Mr. Marks nor his secretary could recall the man's name.

17. Either the night watchman is asleep or the telephone is out of order.

18. Both the reservations and confirmations can be made through this desk.

19. Not only Russell but also his brothers have registered for the contest.

20. Mrs. Thomason asked if the models were ready and if they remembered their instructions.

WORK PROJECT 27

Identifying Dependent Clauses Used as Parts of Speech

A. Each of the following sentences contains a dependent clause. Block it in and identify it as a noun, adjective, or adverb by filling in the sentence patterns or drawing an arrow to the word being modified. For an adverb clause, draw an arrow to the verb in the main clause.

Ex: The printer said | that the pamphlets were finished | .
     (s   v   o (noun))

The stove | which she bought | had to be returned for repairs.
          (ADJ.)

The electricity was cut off | when a tree fell against the line | .
                            (ADV.)

1. Marcella spoke as though she were very tired.

2. The cashier said that the checks would be ready by five o'clock.

3. That I can finish on time is doubtful.

4. Ruth put the stamps where no one can find them.

5. We will accept whatever is available.

6. They were surprised when they saw us.

7. Martin, who had arranged for the transportation, greeted her.

8. You can go with whomever you like.

9. The mechanics rushed the work in order that they could finish before closing time.

10. One reason has been that the soil is infertile.

11. Two trays of bread dropped out when the truck rounded the corner.

12. The vegetables which we offer are of the highest quality.

13. Proceed next to Jones's Store, which is located on Elm Street.

14. He is the man whose records have been missing.

15. Wait for me while I search for coins.

16. Mrs. Percy will sell the farm before she leaves for New York.

17. Let us know immediately if you get the order.

18. Mr. Sturinger resigned so that he could devote himself to art.

19. Miss Flannery won't respond unless you flatter her.

20. Ralph agreed to exchange the tie if I didn't like it.

B. Place commas where they are required in the following sentences. Not all sentences will require comma punctuation.

1. Three insurance claims have already been honored and several more are pending.

2. The laboratory report indicated that she had an infection though there was no visible sign of illness.

3. Can you guess which prize I chose?

4. She has not opened the present since it arrived from Mexico.

5. The consensus of opinion was that a merger would not benefit us.

6. The fishermen demanded a higher price for crab meat before they would even put to sea.

7. We were delayed at the border for two hours since we had to arrange for innoculations.

8. How he could remain so calm was a mystery.

9. The Four-Wheelers which is a local automobile club is sponsoring a two-day drive from California to Oregon.

10. Mr. Sutherland was an immediate success in handling the problems which are peculiar to our firm.

11. The man who will direct the company's research spoke to us briefly.

12. Mr. Edwin is one of those farsighted businessmen who keep abreast of developments in their fields.

13. Both the form and the content of his letter were appealing yet there was something indefinable about Chesterton's style that annoyed me.

14. The Cooks won't return until Thursday because Nell spoke to them last week.

15. The construction was delayed because the storm created a flash flood at the building site.

16. Mr. Pomeroy assumes responsibility for whoever works with him.

17. He carefully adjusted the valve and soon the furnace was operating at normal temperature.

18. That is the Miss Jones whom I interviewed yesterday.

19. We shall refer your inquiry to James Black, Inc. which is an auxiliary branch.

20. Where we could locate another trained engineer was the problem.

21. Mr. Pierson wanted to handle the Williams account personally but other commitments tied his hands.

22. Stacy should concede the election since the returns indicate a landslide for the opposition.

23. We left the meeting while the final vote was being taken.

24. Robert Fillmore lives on Birch Avenue which runs parallel to Brown Street.

25. Are there any grocery stores on the street where you live?

26. The discoloration at the top of the jar indicates that the food has spoiled.

27. There were several gadgets in the drawer though not one looked like a can opener.

28. The salesgirl with whom you discussed the matter referred it to Mr. Brogen.

29. Mr. Burton who is the plaintiff's attorney is waiting to see you.

30. One of the auditors caught the error and corrected it and then the cost analysis was acceptable to Mr. Conant.

C. Make any necessary corrections. Use the preferred form wherever there are two choices.

1. He was not as talkative as usual.

2. It looks like we had a good day.

3. I won't go except you go, too.

4. We must wait for the bell without the instructor grants us special permission to leave early.

5. The clerk will cash your check providing you can show proper identification.

6. He can't help agreeing but that I am the best man for the job.

7. Be sure and try the tamale pie.

8. The sun had no sooner risen but the birds began to sing.

9. These recent figures are not as encouraging as the ones we received last month.

10. She reasons about money like her mother used to reason.

11. Try and visit Yellowstone Park on the journey west.

12. The new dresses are shorter, but not as tightly fitting, as this season's.

13. Please be sure and ask for Howard's Handy Hooks the next time you visit a sporting goods store.

14. She is quicker, but not so accurate, as her sister.

15. I cannot deny but that you have lost weight.

16. I knew Mr. Hill would be sure and ask for me.

17. Jonathan is more serious, but not so perceptive, as Robert.

18. Who could disagree but that the new arrangement is better?

19. It looks like the strike will be averted.

20. Remember and deliver Mr. Postum's order first.

21. What more can I do except to try and correct the mistake?

22. The report can be revised satisfactorily providing the deadline is extended.

23. Mr. Wilson talks like he might transfer his account to us.

24. He couldn't deny but that three men weren't enough for the job.

25. We had no sooner invested the money but the stock market began to drop.

12 VERBALS

Though we have now concluded the parts of speech, there still remains for our attention a special class of words and word groups which are used as parts of speech. These words are called *verbals*. They resemble verbs, but they are used as naming or modifying words rather than as asserting words. Like dependent clauses, they help provide sentence variety and compact more meaning into a sentence.

GERUNDS

A gerund is a verbal ending in *-ing* that is used as a noun. It is derived from a verb but is used to name an action rather than to assert an action. Compare the *-ing* words in these two sentences:

> We *have been talking* for an hour.

> *Talking* is enjoyable.

In the first sentence, *have been talking* is the verb, asserting action. In the second sentence, *talking* is a gerund; it names the action and therefore functions as a noun. Notice that *talking* is an *ing* form of a verb without any helping verbs. By itself it could not be used as a verb.

In addition to serving as a subject, a gerund, like any noun, can also serve as an object, an object of a preposition, or a complement noun:

>   S   V   O
> Mr. Smith stopped the *talking*.

>   O.P.
> We heard them above the *talking*.

>   S   LV   CN
> My reservation about her is her continual *talking*.

PRESENT PARTICIPLES

A *present participle* is a verbal ending in *-ing* that is used as an adjective:

> The talking doll is a delightful toy.

> Henry provided us with a thrilling account of his hiking tour.

The participle gets its name from the fact that it is the same as the present participle form of a verb without any helping words. This breakdown of verb forms for *to ring* should refresh your memory.

PRESENT	PAST	FUTURE	PRESENT PARTICIPLE	PAST PARTICIPLE
ring	rang	will ring	am ringing	have rung

Obviously there is no difference between a gerund and a present participle. For the sake of convenience, an *-ing* verbal used to name an action is called a gerund; an *-ing* verbal used to describe something as being in a state of action is called a present participle.

A one-word participle will occur immediately before the word it modifies or after a linking verb. A present participle will answer the adjective questions *Which one?* and *What kind?*

PAST PARTICIPLES

A *past participle* is a verbal usually ending in *d, ed, n,* or *en.* It is used as an adjective:

The car broke down in a deserted part of the hills.

The torn sleeve had to be mended.

Tom resented Bill's refined manner of speaking.

The broken lever was replaced.

A past participle gets its name from the fact that it is the same as the past participle form of a verb without any helping words:

PRESENT	PAST	FUTURE	PRESENT PARTICIPLE	PAST PARTICIPLE
tear	tore	will tear	am tearing	have torn

A past participle describes something as being in a state in which it has already been acted upon. For example, a *used* towel is one which has already absorbed moisture from the hands of a previous user. Like a present participle, a past participle also occurs immediately before the noun it modifies or after a linking verb. It answers the adjective question *Which one?* and *What kind?*

INFINITIVES

An *infinitive* (*to walk, to go, to sit*) is the form used to designate a verb family: *walk, walked, will walk, has been walking,* etc. An infinitive, however, is itself not used as a verb. Like a noun it may name action; like a present or past participle it may modify a noun; or it may function as an adverb.

    S   LV   CA
To delay was understandable.

    S   V   O
Mr. Hillborn decided *to retire.*

    S   LV   CN
My impulse was *to run.*

The book to borrow is *Gone with the Wind.*   (adjective)

The gambler played cards to win.   (adverb)

An infinitive functioning as a noun will occur in the position of a subject, an object, or a complement noun and will answer the noun question *What?* An infinitive functioning as an adjective will occur after the noun it modifies and will answer the question *Which one?* or *What kind?* An infinitive functioning as an adverb is more flexible in position but normally will occur after the verb or after the basic sentence pattern in an S-V-O sentence.

VERBAL PHRASES

By itself, a verbal is often not sufficient to convey the full meaning of what we wish to say. For instance, the sentence *Sorting is the girls' task* would make sense only if a reader already knew the answer to the question *Sorting what?* A clearer sentence would be *Sorting tomatoes carefully is the girls' task*. Other sentences could be constructed which would give even more meaning to the action *sorting:*

S   LV   CN

[Sorting tomatoes in the shed] was a less rigorous task.

S   LV   CN

[Sorting tomatoes according to three categories] was my job.

Constructions like those blocked off above are called *verbal phrases*. Here is the point to be established: like the verbs from which they are derived, verbals can have objects, complements, and modifiers. An illustration of this point is evident in these two sentences:

S   V   O

Since ten o'clock this morning they *have been sorting* tomatoes in the shed.

S   V

[Sorting tomatoes in the shed] appeals to them.

A verbal phrase functions in much the same manner as a prepositional phrase or a dependent clause. It occurs in the same positions. It is a group of words used as a single part of speech. In the example above, the verbal phrase *Sorting tomatoes in the shed* is a noun used as the subject of the sentence. The key word is *Sorting*, which is a gerund. Here are some additional verbal phrases in which the key word is a gerund:

S   V

For the background music the director preferred

O

[singing without accompaniment] .

O.P.

This candy has a reputation for [spoiling children's appetites] .

S   LV   CN

Johnnie's recreation was [playing in a school band] .

If the key word in a verbal phrase is a present or past participle, then the phrase will function as an adjective, as in these sentences:

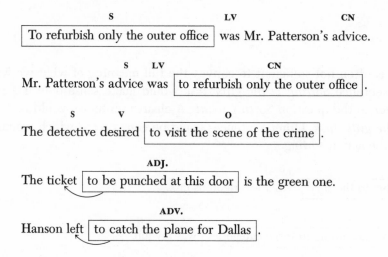

The two men | punching the time clock | are apprentices.

The warehouse | built last year | has not yet been used to capacity.

If the key word in a verbal phrase is an infinitive, then the phrase can be used as a noun, an adjective, or an adverb:

$$
\overset{\textbf{S}}{\boxed{\text{To refurbish only the outer office}}} \quad \overset{\textbf{LV}}{\text{was}} \quad \overset{\textbf{CN}}{\text{Mr. Patterson's advice.}}
$$

$$
\overset{\textbf{S}}{\text{Mr. Patterson's}} \overset{\textbf{LV}}{\text{advice was}} \quad \overset{\textbf{CN}}{\boxed{\text{to refurbish only the outer office}}}.
$$

$$
\overset{\textbf{S}}{\text{The detective}} \overset{\textbf{V}}{\text{desired}} \quad \overset{\textbf{O}}{\boxed{\text{to visit the scene of the crime}}}.
$$

The ticket | to be punched at this door | **ADJ.** is the green one.

Hanson left | to catch the plane for Dallas | **ADV.**.

PUNCTUATING VERBAL PHRASES

All verbal phrases used as nouns or adverbs are considered to be restrictive and do not require comma punctuation. Verbal phrases used as adjectives are considered to be restrictive when they are necessary to identify the nouns they modify. None of the verbal phrases used as examples have thus far required comma punctuation.

Commas are used only with verbal phrases used as nonrestrictive adjectives. The chief principle to keep in mind is the one you have previously utilized in handling dependent clauses: if a modifying phrase is not needed to identify the noun it describes, then it is nonrestrictive. Observe the following pairs of sentences. In each case the first sentence will contain a participial phrase used restrictively, and the second one will contain a participial phrase used nonrestrictively.

The boy *polishing the car* is my son.

Jerry, *polishing the car,* did not look up.

The disc jockey *hired by Mr. Burk* is well known.

Tom Trotter, *hired by Mr. Burk,* is well known.

Sometimes a participial phrase precedes the subject, especially when it is not needed to identify the noun described. When this is the case, the participial phrase is set off in much the same manner as an adverb clause used to introduce the main clause:

Bothered by the noise in the hallway, Dick shut his door.

Seeing the bus, we ran down the street.

ELIMINATING DANGLING MODIFIERS

> *Sweating and panting,* the *top* of the mountain was reached.
>
> *Embarrassed by its lumpiness,* the *sauce* was removed from the table.

These sentences are confusing because they are illogical. The top of the mountain cannot be sweating and panting, and the sauce cannot be embarrased by its lumpiness. In grammatical terms these two verbal phrases are said to dangle. They do not logically modify the words which common sense tells us they must modify. The simplest correction is to change the sentences so that the nouns being modified occur immediately after the verbal modifier:

> *Sweating and panting,* the *hikers* reached the top of the mountain.
>
> *Embarrassed* by its lumpiness, the *hostess* removed the sauce from the table.

Complete Work Project 28

WORK PROJECT 28

**Identifying Verbals Used
as Parts of Speech**

A.   Underline the verbals in the following sentences. Identify them as nouns, adjectives, or adverbs by writing in the sentence patterns or drawing an arrow to the words they modify.

Ex: Her *singing* bothered the *barking* dog.

1.   The creating of the new position has not affected us yet.

2.   Mr. Willard approves of Mildred's acting.

3.   The acting principal handled the disturbed students.

4.   Which network specializes in music broadcasting?

5.   The lasting value of her contribution has become very evident.

6.   A certified check will be sent to you.

7.   Heaven should protect the working girl from divorced men.

8.   The objection to raise is the matter of cost.

9.   One prerequisite is the ability to type.

10.   The typewriter to use is the one behind the counter.

11.   Helen and her husband stopped to visit.

12.   The doctor has one more patient to visit.

13.   He swam in the pool to exercise.

14.   Most of us refused to yield.

15.   The person to reward is the one who conceived this idea.

16.   The old woman was recommended for her cooking and baking.

17.   To interrupt would annoy him.

18.   Broken glass lined the driveway to the street.

19. The smiling athlete said to wait.

20. That unclaimed package has been sitting there all day.

B. Underline the verbal phrases in the following sentences. Identify them as nouns, adjectives, or adverbs by writing in the sentence patterns or by drawing an arrow to the words they modify.

Ex: $\overset{s}{\text{Thinking about the problem}}$ may $\overset{v}{\text{help}}$ $\overset{o}{\text{solve}}$ it.

 $\overset{}{\underline{\text{Filled with a sense of duty}}}$, Mr. $\overset{s}{\text{Matthews}}$ $\overset{v}{\text{decided}}$ $\overset{o}{\text{to run for mayor}}$.

1. Excited about the trip, the children crowded around the counselor.

2. We thanked the man for assembling the model airplane.

3. The ledger lying on my desk is open at the right page.

4. The robbery investigated by the detective has recently been solved.

5. The conditions stipulated in the contract prevent our selling the copyrights.

6. Recognizing the driver, the guard opened the gate.

7. The company provided us with six weeks of school to orient us to our new jobs.

8. To have sustained more lawsuits would have brought our financial ruin.

9. The *Wake Island* is the old freighter to be sold by the government.

10. The agents polled by *Steel Magazine* expect a summer steel strike of six weeks' duration.

C. Insert commas wherever they are needed in the following sentences. Remember that only nonrestrictive verbals require punctuation.

1. Machines to read, translate, think, and correct errors will be discussed at the Annual Western Joint Computer Conference.

2. The Western Management Association will hold a one-day meeting on the problems and costs of administering company health, wealth, and pension programs.

3. Eugene Wengert representing Reynolds & Co. will address the Brockton Kiwanis Club.

4. Convinced of its need in modern times the college has added a special course in jet engines to its aeronautics curriculum.

5. There stood Mr. Bullwinkle making notes in his little black memorandum book.

6. To prove his point the speaker cited an example of the partnership of industry with education.

7. Lockheed Missiles and Space Division at Sunnyvale, California, has an opening for a patent attorney having a background in the field of electronics.

8. Rapid expansion of the market for control computers has been responsible for creating new positions in technical sales management.

9. The New York Stock Exchange reversing its former policy announced a pay-as-you-go investment practice in the securities business.

10. The chapter to be completed in March is titled "Discerning Current Business Trends."

D. Some of the following sentences contain verbal phrases that dangle. Rewrite them in such a manner that the verbal phrase correctly modifies the subject that follows.

Ex: Seeing the child about to be struck, the car applied its brakes.

.... Seeing the child about to be struck, the driver applied his brakes. ....

1. Being concerned over the vanishing elegance of the old city, this statute was passed by the council to prevent further inroads by freeways.

....

....

2. Engaged in basic research, there was no spare time for Mark to handle his committee assignment.

....

....

3. Reporting on the progress of road development in the area, the district engineer commended our decision to install a new lighting system on the bridge.

....

....

4. Expanding and diversifying its production, the growth of the Mayhew Machine Co. is rapid.

....

....

5. Featuring new automatic conveniences, the Morton and Associates will give you pleasing results with its new reflex camera.

....

....

13 CAPITALIZATION

Though capitalization once depended primarily upon the whim of the author, today our habits in capitalizing words have become conventionalized. These conventions are explained and illustrated below. You may already be familiar with most of them, but as you read you should give special attention to those uses which cause you difficulty.

- A capital is used for the *first word* of

Every sentence:
>A customer inquired about the price.
>This letter confirms my telephone call.

Every quotation which expresses a complete thought:
>Mr. Carroll said, "Our new line of dresses will be displayed soon."

>**But**

>He said that his loyalty was "incorruptible."

Every word or phrase used as a complete thought:
>Are you going?   *No.   Of course.   Perhaps.*
>When did you arrive?   *Yesterday.   A week ago.*

The salutation of a letter:
>Dear Sir: Dear Mr. Freeborn:
>My dear John:

The complimentary close of a letter:
>Yours very truly,   Sincerely yours,
>Cordially,   Very sincerely yours,

A passage or sentence independent in meaning from the clause which introduces it:
>In concluding, let me say this: The report proves . . .

>**But**

>The reason for attending college is twofold: to prepare for one of the professions and to gain a sense of culture.

Every line of poetry:

> Alone!
> An old woman in a rocking chair
>   Waiting, waiting—
> When will death ripen?

Every title and every important word in titles of books, magazines, stories, poems, plays, articles, essays, musical compositions, speeches, radio and television programs, and the like:

The Scarlet Letter	"Over There"
Of Human Bondage	"Father Knows Best"
The Call Beyond Time	"How To Make a Million Dollars"
The Wall Street Journal	"My Day"
La Bohème	"Before the Party"
The Sound of Music	"With Malice toward None"

Note 1.   The first and last words of a title are always capitalized. Except when they occur in these positions, prepositions and articles (*a, an, the*) are not capitalized, though it is permissible to capitalize prepositions of six letters or more: "Man *Against* Darkness."

Note 2.   It is becoming increasingly popular to use solid capitals to indicate the titles of books, periodicals, and the like: We read the reviews of THE NAKED EYE in LIFE MAGAZINE.

• A capital is used for every proper noun or adjective derived from a proper noun:

	COMMON NOUN	PROPER NOUN OR ADJECTIVE
Geographical names	That *mountain* looks inaccessible.	*Mt. Everest* looks inaccessible.
	We fell in love with one *state*.	We fell in love with *Colorado*.
	Our *city* is clean.	We cleaned up *Springdale*.
	They left their native *land*.	They left *Sweden*.

Note 1.   Do not capitalize a geographical term used before a name when it is not a part of the name; do not capitalize a geographical term that is used in the plural.

> the Missouri and Mississippi *rivers*
>
> the *valley* of the Mississippi

Note 2.   "City of" and "State of" are preferred in legal documents and commercial papers, but "city of" and "state of" are equally acceptable: "the State of Maine" or "the state of Maine."

Streets, parks, buildings, schools, churches, etc.	A new *senior high school* is to be built soon.	A new *McGrath High School* will be built soon.
	We admired the old *church*.	We admired *St. Paul's Cathedral*.
	Which *street* is repaired?	Is Lincoln Street repaired?
Planets, stars, and constellations	The *planet* is enveloped in vapors.	*Venus*, not *Mars*, is enveloped in vapors.

Compass directions	We headed our station wagon *south*.	(Daylilies thrive in the *South*.)
Names of individuals	A *man* hailed me.	*Martin Crosby* hailed me.
Names of relatives	My *uncle* likes to tease my aunt.	*Uncle Bertram* likes to tease *Aunt Milly*.
Names of companies, institutions, political parties, etc.	I work for a local *foundry*.	I work for *Yuba Erectors*.
	Did you join a *political party?*	Did you join the *Democratic Party?*
	Please attend the next meeting of our *club*.	Please attend the next meeting of the *Big Brothers*.
Names of races, languages, nationalities		*Per Hansa* spoke *Norwegian*. I prefer *French* pastries. The *Englishman* described the *American* way of life.
Days of the week	What *day* did you call?	Was it *Monday* that you called?
Months of the year	She was ill for two *months*.	She was ill during *April* and *May*.
Seasons of the year	He plays *summer* and *winter* sports.	(Only when personified: Has *Winter* touched you with his chill finger?)
Holidays and church days	This company observes *holidays* and some *church days*.	This company observes *Labor Day* and *Good Friday*.
Names of particular ships, trains, planes, etc.	We traveled on a *ship*, a *train*, and a *plane*.	We traveled on the *Lurline*, the *Santa Fe Chief*, and the *Franciscan*.
References to deity	Zeus was the chief *god*.	Worship *God* in your own fashion as long as you keep His commandments.
School subjects	I disliked the course in *mathematics*.	I disliked Mathematics 10 at Vernon City College.
Specialized parts of a work		Act 1, Scene 3 Volume II, Vol. II Unit 5 Book III Article 7 (But: page 101)
Sums of money in legal documents and commercial papers		Six months after date I promise to pay Roger Dent the sum of One Hundred Fifty Dollars.
Titles of rank, office and status	He is an *officer* in the fraternity.	President John Smith and Secretary Bill Olsen conducted the meeting.

It will soon be time to vote for a new *president*.	The *President* granted us an interview. (The President of the United States.)
	The *Pope* appeared on the the balcony. (The current Pope.)
A *minister* and a *professor* addressed the group.	*Reverend William Hartley* and *Professor Hunter Lundigan* addressed the group.
	John Smith, *Jr.* Mollie Gloye, *Ph.D.*

Note.   If the reference is clear, it is allowable to use a capitalized title of rank or office in place of the title plus the proper name:

> *Governor Jackson* will attend the conference . . . The *Governor* said . . . and it was clear that the *Governor* had . . .

Complete Work Project 29

WORK PROJECT 29

Capitalization

Underline each word that should be capitalized.

1. mr. murphy said, "let me have the salt, robert."

2. mathematics, physics, and spanish are my most difficult subjects in college this fall.

3. hubert wrote his first book, *the beginning of the end*, while he was attending huddleston college, which is located in platt city, in eastern ohio.

4. we saw senator bridgman and his family vacationing at lake mercer . . . and later, when we asked him . . . the senator said . . .

5. please stop to see my two friends nell and gwendolyn when you head east on your trip through the midwest.

6. send your contributions to "dollars for blood donors," in care of the national broadcasting company, long island 11, new york.

7. "how to memorize ten words a day" is the article in the current issue of time to which I referred you.

8. this ring would look appropriate on a senator or congressman or fraternity member.

9. this spring we listened to a new record from a blue labels, inc. album entitled "two tramps in mud time."

10. lola morita appeared in the older version of *to live in peace*, which the president requested be shown to the visiting russian diplomats.

11. my aunt advised uncle sorbin to take baby care 10 at northfield adult evening school during the spring term.

12. both the pope and the president agreed on the dangers of nuclear fallout.

13. one year after date I promise to pay John Z. Spratt three hundred forty-nine dollars.

14. in act 1, scene 5, of mr. harrell's new play, *the wink of an eye,* a pope and a president make a plea for sanity and humanity in conducting the affairs of english-speaking nations.

15. "the sink is overflowing," she said; "the water is spilling onto the floor."

16. the president of our club cleared his throat and began as follows: "it has occurred to me that the office of secretary should be filled by a native of the city of oakville and that he should be the kind of man who will say to himself, 'how can I best serve the oakville junior chamber of commerce?' "

17. will you cross the atlantic and pacific oceans on the queen mary and the lurline?

18. in the old testament god commanded the isrealites not to worship any other gods before him.

19. armed forces day parades always command good crowds, but easter and christmas concerts are not well attended.

20. let us wander through the streets

    gentled with rain

    let us shoulder our defeats—

    pain, pain.

14 PUNCTUATION

END MARKS

The marks which are used to separate one sentence from another are sometimes called the end marks.

- A *declarative* sentence (one that states a fact) ends with a period:

    Mr. Roberts is the personnel manager.

- An *imperative* sentence (one that makes a request or gives a command) ends with a period:

    Please resubmit the production report for June.

    Make four copies of the enclosure.

- An *interrogative* sentence (one that asks a question requiring a reply) ends with a question mark:

    When did Mr. Kenan begin working for us?

- An *exclamatory* sentence (one that shows surprise or strong feeling) ends with an exclamation point:

    What a gratifying compliment!

Note. An exclamatory sentence is often a fragment which is punctuated as if it were a complete thought. The sentence above really carries the implication "What a gratifying compliment *that is!*"

Though end punctuation is simple enough to master, there are additional uses of each end mark. Not common sense but knowledge of the accepted conventions is required in determining whether to use one question mark or two after a question concluded with a quoted question. Note the conventions in the following situations.

The Period

If an abbreviation occurs at the end of a sentence, the period following the abbreviation also serves as the end mark:

    The meeting will begin at 2:15 p.m.

    Not

    The meeting will begin at 2:15 p.m. ⊙

- The period is also used as a mark indicating omission, as in abbreviations. An abbreviation is always followed by a period, which indicates that certain letters have been left out. Acceptable abbreviations are outlined below:

  1. Initials, degrees, and titles before or after proper names:

J. F. Kennedy		A.B.	(Bachelor of Arts)
J. Alfred Prufrock		M.A.	(Master of Arts)
Guy M. Sweeney		B.S.	(Bachelor of Science)
Mr.	(Mister)	Ph.D.	(Doctor of Philosophy)
Messrs.	(Messieurs)	D.D.	(Doctor of Divinity)
Mrs.	(Mistress)	M.D.	(Doctor of Medicine)
Mme.	(Madame)		
Mmes.	(Mesdames)		
Dr.	(Doctor)		
Jr.	(Junior)		
Sr.	(Senior)		

  Dr. Johnson examined Mr. D. M. Murchison's injury.

  Harold Burton, Jr., works on the floor above.

  John Carter, Ph.D., will supervise the research.

Note. When a title or degree comes after the proper name, as in the second and third illustrations above, a pair of commas is used to set it off because it is considered to be nonessential to the basic structure of the sentence. It is preferable to spell out *Honorable, Professor, Senator,* and *Reverend.*

  2. Dates, states, and the word *Number:*

A.D.	(In the year of our Lord)	a.m.	(morning)
B.C.	(Before Christ)	p.m.	(afternoon)
No.	(Number)	Calif.	(California)
Nebr.	(Nebraska)	Mo.	(Missouri)

  Diogenes Smith was born in 1910 A.D., not B.C.

  Your new social security card is No. 100-12-4166.

- Except when addressing an envelope or writing a hurried personal note, do not use abbreviations:

  (George)   (Massachusetts)

  ~~Geo.~~ Rutherford's alliance with this firm began in ~~Mass.~~ ten years ago.

- Use a period between dollars and cents expressed in figures. The period is not required in expressing even dollars.

  We are quoting a price of $14.95 for the sweaters and $10 for the slacks.

The Question Mark

- Use a question mark *only* after a direct question:

  Should we relinquish our claim?

  You returned the favor, didn't you?

  Who said, "The addressograph machine is out of order"?

  (These questions require answers.)

Avoid: Mr. Cotton inquired if I had mailed the package ⦸
(This sentence is called an indirection question. It does not require an answer and should therefore be punctuated as a statement.)

- Use a question mark to end a sentence which concludes with a quoted question:

    He looked as though he wanted to say, "What is wrong with me?"

- Use a single question mark after a double question (a quoted question following a question):

    Who said, "When do we open the doors for the sale?"

    Avoid: Who said, "When do we open the doors for the sale?" ⦸

- For emphasis, it is allowable to use the question mark after each item in a series. Used in this fashion the question mark indicates that each item could be expanded into a separate sentence. With this use of the question mark, no capital letter is used except at the beginning of the first question.

    Allowable: Shall I send copies to Mr. Smith? to Miss Harris? to Mr. Bekins?

    More common: Shall I send copies to Mr. Smith, to Miss Harris, and to Mr. Bekins?

- It is sometimes possible to use a question mark in the middle of a sentence:

    A verbal phrase answering the question "which one?" or "what kind?" occurs after the noun it modifies.

    That year (was it 1950?) was the beginning of an extremely profitable association.

The Exclamation Point

- Use an exclamation point after an expression of surprise or strong feeling:

    Goodness! Why did you do that?

    "Let me out of here!" he cried.

- If *oh* introduces an expression of strong feeling, the *oh* is set off by a comma, and the exclamation point occurs at the end of the sentence:

    Oh, that goes without saying!

- Never use more than one exclamation point after a sentence:

    We never dreamed of doing so well!

    Avoid: We never dreamed of doing so well! ⦸

Complete Work Project 30

THE COMMA

The comma is a mark of separation used to point out the grouping of words, phrases, and clauses with respect to the grammatical structure of a sentence. Viewed less technically, it is a mark which helps the reader distinguish the main thought from material that stands apart from it or interrupts it. In this sense the comma is also an important guide to inflection when we are reading aloud.

Your grasp of word order will help you see immediately what is wrong with the comma punctuation in the following sentences. A comma should not be used to separate the essential parts of a sentence pattern or to interrupt normal word order. Read through this list carefully before proceeding to the first generalization for using the comma acceptably.

Avoid

S　　　　V　　　O
The prospector⌒ revised his list of commodities.

S　　　　　　　　　　　(v)　　　(v)　　　V
│ How he won control of the company │⌒ has never been ascertained.

S　　　　　　　　LV　　　　CN
│ Seeing too much good in others │⌒ is hardly a defect.

S　V　　　　　　　O
He said⌒│ that the revision would be accurate │.

S　　V　　　　　　　O
She asked⌒│ if the letters had been signed │.

S　　　　V　　　　　O
Mr. Tarman disliked⌒│ refusing credit to anyone │.

The second proposal was generous⌒ and acceptable.
(two words connected by a conjunction)

S　LV　　　　　CN
My opinion is⌒│ that the delay was not justifiable │.

S　LV　　　　　CN
The chief economy is⌒ the quick processing of applications.

A tall, good-looking⌒ man stepped up to her counter.

S　　　S　　　S　　V
Every man, woman, and child⌒ can benefit from the new plan.

Mr. Burns accepted the explanation⌒│ for the error │.

The display was interesting, but⌒ it contained nothing new.
(The conjunction *but* introduces the main clause.)

One-comma Punctuation

One-comma punctuation indicates that the material preceding or following the comma is considered to be separate from the rest of the sentence or from another part of the sentence. There are five general kinds of separation. Many of the illustrations of these five principles are traditionally listed as individual rules for using the comma. For convenience, a brief explanation of this traditional rule is included in parentheses.

• A comma is used to separate a part of the sentence which is independent of the main thought.

    Mr. Smith completed the transaction.　　(main thought)

    Yes, *Mr. Smith completed the transaction.*　　(*yes* or *no* at beginning of a sentence)

    Well, *Mr. Smith finally completed the transaction.*

                                (mild interjection at beginning of a sentence)

Marie, *Mr. Smith completed the transaction.*   (noun in direct address)
   Mr. Smith completed the transaction, Marie.

She said, *"Mr. Smith completed the transaction."*   (words identifying the speaker)
   "Mr. Smith completed the transaction," she said.

Of course, *Mr. Smith completed the transaction.*
                                       (parenthetical expression at beginning of a sentence)

- A comma is used to separate words, phrases, and clauses of equal grammatical weight.

> We hired *carpenters, plumbers,* and *bricklayers.*   (words in a series)
>
> The manager accepted applications *in the spring, in the fall,* and *during busy periods.*
>   (phrases in a series)
>
> The president *considered my suggestion, reversed his former decision,* and *formulated a new policy.*   (predicates in a series)
>
> The buyer knew *that the rains would soon begin, that umbrellas would be in demand,* and *that our supply would be depleted.*   (dependent clauses in a series)
>
> Mr. Hill asked for my opinion, but he followed John's advice.
>   (two main clauses joined by a conjunction)
>
> The company wanted only *reliable, competent* salesmen.   (coordinate adjectives)

Coordinate adjectives require additional explanation. In the example above, *reliable* and *competent* are both adjectives that refer directly to the same noun. Their order could be reversed without changing the meaning: *competent, reliable* salesmen. Another test for the correctness of the comma is to substitute for it the word *and.* Notice that this substitution will sound natural: reliable *and* competent salesmen.

Not all adjectives preceding a noun need to be separated, however:

> It was a spacious old warehouse.
>
> The office was furnished with several large lounging chairs.

In these examples, notice that it would be impossible to say *spacious and old* or *several and large and lounging chairs.*

A recommended practice is to omit the comma with numerals and with common adjectives of size and age:

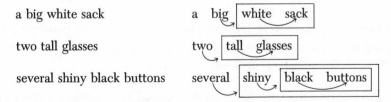

- A comma is used to separate a sentence part which has been shifted from its usual sentence position for use as an introductory element.

> Because the fire had started mysteriously, an investigation was begun. (An investigation was begun because the fire had started mysteriously.)
>
> To satisfy my conscience, I contributed another quarter to the coffee fund. (I contributed another quarter to the coffee fund to satisfy my conscience.)

In both examples the adverb (a dependent clause and an infinitive phrase) has been shifted from its normal position following the main clause.

- A comma is used to separate a nonrestrictive sentence part which precedes or follows the main clause.

> *Mr. Smith completed the transaction,* although he was reluctant to do so.
>
> *Mr. Smith appointed Howard,* who had always wanted the position.
>
> *Mr. Smith preferred Boswell and Son,* who he believed rendered good service.
>
> *Mr. Smith decided on Tuff-board,* a local product.
>
> Complaining about her discomfort, *the woman entered the waiting room.*
>
> Disappointed by Mr. Merton's lack of enthusiasm, *Miss Tanovitz withdrew her suggestion.*

In all the above examples, the sentence parts printed in roman type are modifiers which are nonessential to our understanding of the main clause.

Even when they occur after the main clause, adverb clauses beginning with (1) *though* and *although* (2)*since* and *as* meaning *because* and (3) *because* when it merely gives evidence for a statement, are set off by comma punctuation.

Adjective clauses which are not necessary to identify the words they modify are set off by comma punctuation, as in the second and third examples.

Verbal phrases which are not necessary to identify the words they modify are set off by comma punctuation, as in the fifth and sixth examples.

When they are nonrestrictive, as in the fourth example, appositives are set off by comma punctuation. An appositive is an equivalent word or word group that repeats the meaning of the word or word group it follows. An appositive can be restrictive or nonrestrictive. Here are some additional illustrations of restrictive and nonrestrictive appositives:

> I was accompanied to the dance by my friend *Harold.*
> (The speaker has more than one friend; the word *Harold* is required to identify which friend.)
>
> I was accompanied to the dance by my best friend, *Harold.*
> (The speaker has only one best friend; the word *Harold* is not required to identify which friend.)

- A comma is used as a courtesy mark to separate sentence parts which might otherwise confuse the reader.

> As of May, 1962, there were 1,498 employees working at our foundry in Austin, Texas.
>
> Saturday, August 4, 1961, is a day I will always remember, for it was then that we first moved into the little cottage at 117 Bellevue, Clinton, Iowa.

The sentences above contain dates, numbers, and geographical names or addresses that require separation into units for convenient reading. Numbers are set off from the left by threes: 12, 114, 807; 29,008; 100,000. Dates are separated according to the day of the week, the day of the month, and the year. Frequently only the month and year are used (April, 1866). Geographical names or addresses are separated according to street number, city, state, and country. When a geographical name or date contains two or more units, the last unit is always separated from the remainder of the sentence:

> December 3, 1740, was the day set aside for signing the treaty.
>
> The new branch office in Springfield, Missouri, is now open.

Occasionally a comma is needed to prevent misreading:

> In hurrying, the women forgot their packages.
> (In hurrying the women?)

> Below, the seagulls were bobbing in the water.
> (Below the seagulls?)

Complete Work Project 31

Two-comma Punctuation

Commas used in pairs enclose material that interrupts the normal word order in the sentence patterns, especially that of the main thought. The interrupting material may be nonessential to the main thought (Mr. Smith, *I believe,* completed the transaction) or it may be a sentence part shifted from its usual position (Mr. Smith, *before he left for France,* completed the transaction).

A good many of the illustrations below were previously encountered in the explanation of one-comma punctuation. Formerly they were set off when they occurred before or after the main thought. Now they are being set off with two commas because they are inserted within the main thought.

> *Mr. Smith,* not Mr. Brown, *completed the transaction.*   (contrast)

> *Mr. Smith,* realizing the urgency, *completed the transaction.* (nonrestrictive verbal phrase)

> *Mr. Smith,* delayed by personal illness, *finally completed the transaction.*
> (nonrestrictive verbal phrase)

> *Mr. Smith,* who is our lawyer, *completed the transaction.*   (nonrestrictive adjective clause)

> *Mr. Smith,* to end the year properly, *completed the transaction.*   (shifted verbal phrase)

> *Mr. Smith,* when he received the letter, *completed the transaction.* (shifted adverb clause)

> *Mr. Smith,* with a gesture of impatience, *completed the transaction.*
> (shifted prepositional phrase)

> *Mr. Smith,* of course, *completed the transaction.*   (parenthetical expression)

> *Mr. Smith,* weary of delay, *completed the transaction.*   (nonrestrictive adjective phrase)

> *Mr. Smith,* the man with the cigar, *completed the transaction.* (nonrestrictive appositive)

> *I said,* Myrna, *that Mr. Smith completed the transaction.*   (noun in direct address)

> "*Mr. Smith,*" she said, "*completed the transaction.*"   (words identifying the speaker)

> *Mr. Smith,* tired and anxious, *completed the transaction.*   (shifted adjectives)

> *Mr. Smith's heirs,* especially his son Luther, *urged him to complete the transaction.*
> (qualifying expression)

Complete Work Project 32

THE COLON

The colon is a linking mark of punctuation. It links the main thought with material that more specifically explains the main thought. In this sense it functions more or less like an equal-sign. In typewriting, a double space is left between the colon and the material it anticipates.

• Use a colon to introduce a list of particulars, an explanation, or a formal quotation consisting of several sentences.

> Almost every personnel manager I know still hopes for three old-fashioned virtues in applicants: competence, reliability, and friendliness.
> (three virtues = competence, reliability, friendliness)

> He had two alternatives: to buy the building or move his office to another location.
> (two alternatives = to buy . . . or move)

> The labor-management battle over the effects of automation of jobs is being complicated by a new struggle: the even faster move of late toward automation abroad than in America, long considered its home.
> (new struggle = faster move toward automation)

> Increased competition with foreign companies that have been mechanizing brings another factor into focus: a country's productivity is now measured by the amount of goods turned out per man hour of labor.

> The president of the Bureau of Advertising summarized his speech as follows: "The research shows that newspapers enjoy a unique position in the daily life of Americans. Most important for the advertiser, it shows that newspaper advertising shares the intimate, immediate personal character of the paper itself. People accept it as factual and down-to-earth. They feel it speaks to them."

A colon throws the emphasis forward toward the material following it. A colon is used at the end of a completed sentence pattern. For that reason the sentence below is not correctly punctuated.

> S   LV
> The chief economic goals in underdeveloped countries are ⊙
>
> CN   CN
> automation and mass production.

• As a routine mark of punctuation, a colon is used (1) after the saluation of a letter and (2) between the hours and minutes when time is expressed in figures.

> Dear Sir: Dear Mrs. Smith: Gentlemen:

> My appointment was scheduled for 2:30 p.m.
> (**But:**   I kept my appointment at two-thirty.)

Complete Work Project 33

THE DASH

In typing, a dash is formed by striking the hyphen twice. No space is left between the hyphens or before or after the dash.

• Use a dash to set off details or particulars which occur before the main thought:

> Bricks, limestone blocks, and sandstone—these are the usual building materials in this part of the country.

> Harriet Anderson and Bibi Daniels—these girls are my nominations for president and vice-president respectively.

Like the colon, the dash is a linking mark of punctuation when used in this fashion. It joins material explaining something in the main thought to the main thought itself. Stylistically the dash throws the emphasis back on the explanatory particulars, whereas the colon throws the emphasis toward what follows it. Compare the same sentence punctuated with a colon and with a dash:

>All these items are on sale: stoves, refrigerators, and washing machines.

>Stoves, refrigerators, and washing machines—all these items are on sale.

• Use dashes instead of commas to set off nonrestrictive appositives which interrupt the main thought:

>Three fruits, apples, pears, and persimmons, are in plentiful supply. (Unclear: three fruits or six fruits?)

>Three fruits—apples, pears, and persimmons—are in plentiful supply.

• Use a dash to indicate a sudden, abrupt break in thought or structure. Used in this fashion, the dash might be called a stop-and-start-again mark of punctuation. It is still a linking mark, however, for the material following it is considered to be an unexpected addition to the material preceding it.

>Mr. Appleby requested that you—but I'll do it for you.

>Where is—oh, there you are!

• Use a dash before an expression such as *namely, for instance, that is,* etc.:

>Hans has one thing to recommend him—namely, his fine sensitivity to common-man tastes.

>Your speech should be concluded at the crucial moment—that is, when bald heads begin nodding.

• For greater emphasis and variety, the dash can be substituted for the comma, but such a substitution should be used sparingly:

>The agreement has been made—and I am going to keep my word.

>One of our employees—Miss Stevens—has won the Courtesy Award.

>Harold—without a bit of help from any of us—has engineered a wonderful advertising campaign.

• Use a dash to set off a final appositive:

>There was only one salesman who could have told a joke like that—Joe Bowman.

>Only two cities offer all the things I am looking for—New York and San Francisco.

• Use a dash before the name of a work or the author when it follows a quoted extract:

>"A woman's chastity is a sty in the devil's eye."—Ingmar Bergman

>"My destiny mended here, not yours."—*Walden*

PARENTHESES

• Use parentheses to enclose material that has an indirect bearing on the main thought but could not be incorporated into the sentence directly without causing an awkward break in structure. Usually such material will be unemphatic in nature:

>Mr. Carter was transferred to Springfield (Missouri, not Ohio) last year.

>My acting (I last appeared in *Hamlet*) has been a constant source of amusement to my wife.

>If you can meet him at the station (the train arrives at five o'clock, doesn't it?), Harry will be waiting in a blue convertible.

- Use parentheses to enclose the numbers or letters used to indicate items being enumerated within a sentence:

> Your autobiographical sketch should emphasize three areas: (1) your training, (2) your former employment, and (3) your future goals.

> The report will include (a) the revised cost estimates, (b) the modified specifications, and (c) a tentative time schedule for completing the preject.

Complete Work Project 34

THE HYPHEN

The best recommendation for learning to use the hyphen in forming compound words is to look up each word in the dictionary and keep its spelling in mind! It is the history of most such words to begin as two separate words, then to become hyphenated, and finally to be written as one word: mail man, mail-man, mailman. Not all words have followed this process; even among those that have, some have advanced at a quicker rate than others. It is possible to list more than a dozen different bases for forming hyphenated words, yet there would be many exceptions within each category. The generalizations offered below are perhaps the most useful ones.

- Use a hyphen with two or more words to form compound words that are not yet spelled as one word:

passer-by	merry-go-round
has-been	secretary-treasurer
son-in-law	step-son
do-nothing	penny-pincher

- In general, use a hyphen with the following prefixes and suffixes:

all-American	allover
anti-Communist	antiwar
ex-mayor	
governor-*elect*	
great-uncle	
half-baked	halfway
pre-election	
pro-United Nations	proslavery
quarter-final	quarterback
self-love	selfsame
un-American	undemocratic
vice-principal	viceregent

- Use a hyphen with two or more words forming a compound adjective before a noun unless the first word ends in *ly:*

good-looking man	well-dressed woman
slow-moving car	up-to-date information

But: coldly worded note
newly introduced slogan
freshly painted sign

- Such words are not hyphenated if they come after the noun:

> well-designed kitchen
>
> **But:** The kitchen was well designed.
>
> an up-to-date report
>
> **But:** The report was up to date.

- Use a hyphen to prevent an awkward combination of vowels or consonants, or to distinguish between different words that would otherwise be spelled and pronounced the same:

anti-intellectual	recollect (to recall)
pre-eminent	re-collect (to collect again)
shell-like	recover (to get back)
cross-stitch	re-cover (to cover again)

Note.   In printed matter, the dieresis mark is often used instead of the hyphen: preëminent, coöperative.

- Use a hyphen with compound numbers from twenty-one through ninety-nine; with written fractions used as adjectives; and with compound written numbers used to express time:

> forty-eight   one hundred twenty-two   one ten-thousandth
>
> a two-thirds majority
>
> **But:** two thirds of the votes
>
> Shall we meet at *two-thirty?*
>
> **But:** We agreed to meet at 2:30 p.m.

- Use a hyphen to indicate the division of a word at the end of a line:

> Most of these so-called critics of the govern-
> ment simply do not know what is involved.

Note.   For a full discussion of this use of the hyphen, see the section on word division.

ITALICS (Underlining)

In printed matter italics are identified by a distinctive type that slants upward to the right. In handwriting or typing, however, italics must be indicated by underlining. Though quotation marks and italics can be used to cover many of the same functions, the modern trend is toward using italics whenever possible.

- Use italics to indicate the titles of books, long poems, plays, musical productions, magazines, newspapers, works of art, and the names of ships, trains, and airplanes:

> *Gone with the Wind* may well endure as the classic novel about the old South.
>
> Have you seen Rodin's famous sculpture *The Thinker?*
>
> It took me hours to read John Milton's most famous poem, *Paradise Lost.*
>
> Have you seen *My Fair Lady?*
>
> The San Francisco *Examiner* is a rival of the San Franciso *Chronicle.*
>
> We could hardly wait for the *Lurline* to drop anchor!
>
> The *Reader's Digest* was the source of most of her ideas.

- Use italics to indicate foreign words which have not yet become Anglicized:

> The other guests were grateful each time he nodded and said *bonjour*.

> A *coup d'état* in a Latin American country is almost certain to be followed by wavering stocks on Wall Street.

Note.   Consult a dictionary whenever you are in doubt about a word's standing.

- Use italics to indicate words, letters, or figures used as such:

> His *2's* were quite similar to his capital *Q's*.

> The word *dame* is the basis for many puns.

> Be sure to distinguish between *to, too,* and *two*.

- Use italics to give a word special stress.

> "He was *not* here," she said again, quietly but firmly.

Note.   Using italics to achieve special emphasis is a device that should be used very sparingly.

THE APOSTROPHE

- Use an apostrophe to form the possessive case of a noun:

A noun not already ending in an *s* adds *'s:*

a man's word	men's wear	John's decision
one week's time	Sue's reply	my son-in-law's tie

A noun already ending in an *s* merely adds the apostrophe:

two girls' sweaters	Mr. Jones' account	ladies' gloves
three weeks' time	boys' clothing	the lads' pets

Note.   For a full discussion of possessive nouns, see pp. 25–27.

- Use an apostrophe to form the plurals of numbers, letters, and words used out of context:

> How many *r's* are there in the word *embarrass?*

> Your *Q's* look like *2's*.

> It is ineffective to throw too many *also's* into your writing.

- Use an apostrophe to indicate contractions:

aren't (are not)	I'll (I will or I shall)
can't (can not)	won't (will not)
don't (do not)	wouldn't (would not)
doesn't (does not)	you're (you are)
it's (it is)	

THE SEMICOLON

Like the comma, the semicolon is a separating mark of punctuation. It indicates a much stronger separation of parts than the comma but a lesser degree than the period. Chiefly it is used to separate two closely related main clauses, though it is also used to separate sentence parts that already contain internal punctuation.

- Use a semicolon to separate two closely related main clauses not joined by a coordinate conjunction:

    Winter sales were fair; spring sales were slightly improved.

    It was too late to get back into the building; the custodian had locked up and left.

The following conjunctive adverbs are commonly used to show a logical connection between two independent thoughts. They are special words—half adverb, half conjunction—which are preceded by a semicolon and followed by a comma:

    The car is still functioning; therefore, I can use it as a trade-in for a newer model.

    Your qualifications seem excellent; however, you must first be interviewed by Mr. Hall.

    I grant you that the mistake was yours; nevertheless, we are willing to replace the part at wholesale price.

Other conjunctive adverbs are these:

accordingly	consequently	besides
at least	moreover	still
in fact	indeed	furthermore

- Use a semicolon to set off the units of a series if one or more of the units contain commas:

    We were assigned to read three books: *The Far Hills,* by Henry Greene; *Looking Homeward,* by M. O. Daugherty; and *The Beacon,* by Alice Farr.

    We agreed that a reorganization was in order; that, if possible, the positions of secretary and treasurer should be combined; and that John Eckhart, a lawyer, should draft a new consitution.

    Your reassignment will take you to Chicago, Illinois; Atlanta, Georgia; or Buffalo, New York.

- Use a semicolon instead of a comma before a coordinate conjunction when one or both the clauses it joins contain internal punctuation, especially when the coordinate conjunction might fail to signify the beginning of a new clause:

    If you take your vacation this week, there will be no one left to take dictation except Joan; and Mildred, as you know, will be unusually busy this month with her own work.

    Because of the repairs being made, Room 66 and its function will be lost to us for two days; and for the next three days, I am afraid, the cafeteria will have to remain closed.

ELLIPSIS MARKS

Ellipsis marks are made on a typewriter by striking the period key three times in succession or four times in succession, depending on the function of the ellipsis marks required. No space is left before or after the ellipsis marks unless a new sentence is begun. Then leave two spaces after the final dot.

- To signify the omission of material at the beginning of a quoted sentence, use three spaced dots; for an omission that occurs internally, use three spaced dots; for an omission at the end of the sentence, use four spaced dots:

    "These anti-intellectual right-wingers, it seems to me, are unconsciously operating on the theory that there is such a thing as a safe idea, a theory that certainly runs counter to our historical tradition of free and open inquiry." (original quotation quoted complete)

    I agree that these people ". . . are unconsciously operating on the theory that there is such a thing as a safe idea, a theory that certainly runs counter to our historical tradition of free and open inquiry." (omission at the beginning of a quoted sentence)

"These anti-intellectual right-wingers . . . are unconsciously operating on the theory that there is such a thing as a safe idea, a theory that certainly runs counter to our historical tradition of free and open inquiry." (omission internally)

"These anti-intellectual right-wingers, it seems to me, are unconsciously operating on the theory that there is such a thing as a safe idea. . . ." (omission at the end of the sentence)

BRACKETS

The typewriter keyboard does not contain a key for brackets. Though it is possible to form them by using the diagonal and hyphen keys, the process is tedious. Most secretaries prefer to leave a space before and after the material to be enclosed and later pen in the brackets.

• Use brackets to enclose material that is inserted into a quoted extract. Often such material takes the form of an editor's note or a correction:

"The gist of his [Thoreau's] meaning was that spiritual values are more important than material possessions."—Extract from a student paper

"In my day [around 1900] a young man felt fortunate indeed if he could work fourteen hours a day and earn a dollar!"—Henry Fuller

Complete Work Project 35

QUOTATION MARKS

• Use quotation marks to enclose a direct quotation:

Mr. Marquis said, "We shall see."

"Where is the mailing room?" asked Miss Hagerty. "I am eager to go to work."

One rule book says, "Never return the serve until your partner has indicated he is ready."

• Do not put quotation marks around an indirect quotation:

Wrong: She asked "how many had their work completed."
Right: She asked how many had their work completed.
          She asked, "How many of you have your work completed?"

• If a quoted statement is interrupted, use quotation marks to set off the quoted material from the rest of the sentence:

"Where I live," said Robert, "there is very little noise."

"One of my errors," confessed Miss Curtis, "was failing to realize my confusion. Now I have wasted an hour's work."

Note.   When a quotation is interrupted, the second part of the quotation is not capitalized unless is begins with a proper noun or the pronoun *I.*

• A quotation running to four lines or more may be single-spaced and indented five spaces from both the right- and left-hand margins. No quotation marks are necessary.

Finally, here is a paragraph from Mr. Blarney's last letter. I don't agree with him. Do you?

> One of my worries has been that our agency commission is too high. Fifteen per cent gives us only a modest return for our labor, I realize, but similar services rendered by similar businesses are much less dear. Couldn't we find a way to reduce our overhead and trim our staff? Please send me your response as soon as you have reflected on this problem.

- When several paragraphs are being quoted, use quotation marks at the beginning of each paragraph and at the end of the final paragraph. If the paragraphs are single-spaced and indented from both margins, no quotation marks are necessary.

"..

....

....

"..

....

....

....

"..

....

.... "

- In reporting dialogue or conversation, each direct quotation should be indented as a paragraph:

> Here is my recollection of our conversation last evening.
>
> "Mr. Durgess," I said, "can you give me the treasurer's report for June for Mr. Yee?"
>
> "Juniper Mystery? What an odd name!" he replied.
>
> "Mr. Durgess, you need to have your hearing checked," I suggested.
>
> "I don't like herring," he said—and hung up.

- No punctuation is required after the explanatory words if the quotation is very brief, especially if the sentence continues beyond the quotation:

> He said "Thanks" and boarded the train.
>
> She yelled "Stop it!" and left the room.

- When a quotation is interrupted between two main clauses closely related in meaning, use a semicolon after the explanatory words. Do not capitalize the first word in the following clause unless it begins with a proper noun or the pronoun *I:*

> "This one is for you," said Margaret; "that one is for Harry."

- A comma or a period is *always* placed inside the quotation mark. A semicolon or a colon *always* occurs outside the quotation mark unless it is a part of the quoted material. A question mark or an exclamation mark belongs inside or outside the quotation mark, depending on its function as a part of the quotation itself or the whole sentence.

> "Yes," he sighed, "today is Monday."
>
> Mr. Weeks called the lay-off a "vacation"; I call it financial disaster.

Mr. Karlson had on exhibit three "humdingers": a three-pound perch, a ten-pound bass, and a huge sand shark.

She asked, "When shall we leave?"

Who was it who said, "Where is my ticket?"

Ralph exclaimed, "It's too cold in there!"

It was good of my wife to say, "Don't bother with the dishes"!

• Use single quotation marks to enclose a quotation within a quotation:

She replied, "Remember Mother's advice, 'If in doubt, do nothing.' "

Note. The end punctuation for the sentence quoted within a quotation also serves for the entire sentence.

• Use quotation marks to set off a dictionary definition:

My dictionary defines *sneer* as "a dog's grin."

• Use quotation marks to enclose the titles of magazine articles, short stories, essays, poems, editorials, songs, and chapters in books when all of these are clearly subdivisions of larger bodies of writing:

"How the Population Explosion Is Affecting Business" is the chief article in this month's issue of *Business Trends*.

The second edition of *Applied Economics* will contain the essay "Product Financing" and also an introduction entitled "The Nature of Economics."

The last chapter of *Modern Business* is called "The Crystal Ball."

Her favorite poem is "The Road Not Taken," by Robert Frost.

Complete Work Project 36

WORK PROJECT 30

Using the End Marks

A. Use the appropriate end marks for the following sentences.

1. Was Reverend Tillsbury successful in his fund drive

2. She asked if the type had been cleaned recently

3. The initiation was held last Wednesday evening, wasn't it

4. Please help me if you have time

5. Rush to the polls and vote for our candidate

6. How fortunate that you remembered the numbers on your ticket

7. Mr. Seldon seldom comes to work before nine o'clock

8. How considerate of them to remember us on our anniversary

9. They asked whether or not we could supply them with leather accessories

10. Have you recalled the jist of the telephone conversation

B. End marks and special situations involving the period, the question mark, and the exclamation mark. Supply the necessary marks.

1. John Holden, M D , is on the other line, Mr Carew

2. Who remarked, "Has she any talent "

3. Henry asked if the order could be filled before 2:15 p m

4. The letter recommended we consult Henry Soames, Sr

5. Jeanette exclaimed, "Oh I didn't see you standing there "

6. Mr. Barnett asked when I would receive my M A degree

7. "How ungrateful you are " yelled the old man

8. Have you seen Roger Barnes lately, or is he still living in your neighborhood, Mrs Hoopes

9. She said quietly, "Where have you been "

10. Ervin Edwards, Jr , verified the date of the manuscript as 147 A D

11. The envelope was addressed to Mmes David and Marcel Lebost

12. I am wondering if his license is No 133-55 or No 188-55

13. Miss Carruthers and her sister, Mrs Brownley, recommended Amos Borden, Ph D

14. Mr and Mrs Wm Gordon
148 Telham Ave
Rainbird, Wash

15. Your price of $12 10 is quite a saving in view of the $15 you were asking last week

C.   Make necessary corrections in the following sentences. If there is an alternate way of punctuating a given sentence, so indicate.

Ex: I asked where she had gone̸.

1. Did she say, "Where is the filing cabinet" ?

2. I found this wallet first, so there! !

3. Miss Coleman meant to say 2:15 pm. instead of 3:15 pm. .

4. I saw Wm. Sawyers talking to Geo. Hazelton, PhD.

5. Miss Branson asked if she were free to leave at four o'clock?

6. We can place these articles on sale for no less than $56.00.

7. Have we had a reply from The Sign Post, or Smith's Store, or the Treasure Chest?

8. Shall we address the account to his office? to his home? or to his ship?

9. Who said, "Why should we continue to wait for Bill?"?

10. Oh! never mind!

WORK PROJECT 31

Using Comma Punctuation

Place commas wherever they are required in the following sentences. Some sentences may not require comma punctuation.

A. Using a comma to set off sentence parts which are independent of the main thought.

1. No the order hasn't arrived Mr. Johnson.

2. Well perhaps the material can be re-ordered.

3. That yardage is on sale isn't it?

4. Yes Miss Cole that receipt will be mailed to you.

5. Mr. Billings handed me the paper and said "Check my addition Larry."

6. Denice said quietly "Mr. Holman won't like that."

7. Oh there he goes!

8. He replied "Yes I understand your brother's problems."

9. Mr. Perkins used to work in this office didn't he?

10. Hugh said "Yes I am to work on the Fuller account am I not?"

B. Using a comma to set off words, phrases, or clauses of equal grammatical weight.

1. Cadillacs Buicks and Chevrolets filled the parking lot.

2. The horse tossed his head ran across the meadow and jumped the fence.

3. Albert is a talented confident reliable design artist.

4. Most cigarette advertisements are stereotyped but occasionally one comes along that contains imagination.

5. The interviewer asked what I had been trained to do and where I had worked previously.

6. Flowers had been placed on the table the mantlepiece and the bookcase.

7. Mr. Todd and Mr. Guthrie are good bosses for they have a direct friendly approach in dealing with others.

8. We tried to avoid a ruinous price war and we were successful.

9. The delivery trucks should be serviced and cleaned and the courtesy car should be repaired.

10. Our clerks ignored Mrs. Rippup's sharp insinuating remarks yesterday because she is usually a very pleasant customer to wait on.

C.   Using a comma to set off a sentence part that has been shifted from its normal position for use as an introductory element.

1. Although the typewriter has been repaired it still does not work properly.

2. If you can't read my writing ask me for help.

3. To qualify for the nomination you must be over forty years old.

4. When you have been here as long as I have you will begin to know something about human nature.

5. To help you assimilate this information I am preparing a series of weekly sales meetings.

6. While there is still time can you modify this design for the left wing of the restaurant?

7. To preserve the original coloring dry in a shaded area.

8. Since the toys are defective they should be returned to us for a refund.

9. Until the dispute is settled the crab boats will remain in the harbor.

10. To obtain the best results with this shampoo make two applications and rub in thoroughly each time.

D.   Using a comma to separate a nonrestrictive sentence part which comes before or after the main thought.

1. Encouraged by his success Mr. Thomas decided to expand his business.

2. Seeing the taxi pull up the reporters rushed forward.

3. There stood Benny filling his plate for the third time.

4. We were able to talk to the eldest son Robert, Jr.

5. Having encountered this difficulty before I believe I know how to solve it.

6. Please cancel my appointment with Mr. Taraval whom I was to have seen at one o'clock today.

7. The sacks of fertilizer arrived in a damaged condition although they had been re-coopered twice.

8. May I direct your attention to Johnson and Johnson a local firm which could benefit from your patronage.

9. Maud Greenway introduced her assistant Joan Maughm.

10. Hearing a loud commotion the foreman ran toward the shop.

E. Using a comma to separate sentence parts which might otherwise confuse the reader.

1. Outside the wind was blowing.

2. In 1954 $176599 was set aside for the expansion of the new factory.

3. The conference is scheduled for Thursday morning August 11 in the Venetian Room Statler Hotel New York City.

4. Below the children were playing on the beach.

5. May 1960 was to have been the completion date for the project, but since then our energies have been diverted to another project at Arrow River Wyoming.

6. Harbert reported a total of 1885 work hours lost through absenteeism.

7. Harbor Maine will be the site for of our newest branch.

8. In transcribing Mary left out an entire paragraph of Mr. Hobbs' dictation.

9. Before leaving the custodian checks the locks on all the doors and windows.

10. Please send the gift certificate to the following: Mr. Burton Randolph 8100 Grand Avenue Kansas City 11 Missouri.

WORK PROJECT 32

Two-comma Punctuation

The following sentences call for commas to be used in pairs to set off interrupting material.

1. Directors of Pacific Power and Light Co. in a surprise move recommended a two-for-one split of the company's common stock.

2. Your credit card if you have been using one will no longer be considered evidence of deductible business expenses.

3. The Securities and Exchange Commission set up after the congressional probe in 1933–34 is keeping a close watch over the securities markets.

4. It was Mr. Rosefield not Mr. Chapley who prepared the income tax return.

5. Matthew T. Dooley representing the Laundry and Linen Supply Board of San Merino testified in favor of the Public Utilities Commission regulation.

6. The commission's staff counsel Frank G. Campbell who favors regulation of the state's production and transmission of natural gas refrained from comment.

7. These truck tires to give maximum wear should be rotated regularly.

8. Several stockholders have in the past demanded their rights as voters.

9. The program director tough and independent resented interference from any quarter.

10. The arrangement though it is without precedent should meet little resistance.

11. The combined assets of the two banks are as I recall about $245 million.

12. "A Christmas bonus of one month's salary" he said "will be given each employee who has been with us for over a year."

13. Unilever Ltd. stocks which were listed only Tuesday have already received warm praise from stock market letter writers.

14. P. F. Burgdoff who has been appointed credit manager of Shell Oil Company's San Francisco division will succeed Richard A. Tompkins a former boss at the end of this month.

15. Her only excuse that she had missed the bus didn't seem plausible.

16. A research and development engineer if we could afford one would make a valuable addition to our staff.

17. Miss Hawly in her desire to finish early left out one of the enclosures.

18. One of the field workers not the supervisor made the recommendation.

19. My first business venture as you will recall was not entirely without mishap.

20. Stock exchanges since the inquiry started have tightened their rules for trading and for admittance of stocks to listing.

21. Elsie whom we are fond of always gives parties which we can't stand.

22. The hydramatic automobile before it could substantiate the firm's claims would have to sell for no more than $1200.

23. No dividends however have as yet been declared.

24. Mr. Church arising from his seat asked to speak.

25. I asked Melvin whose work was already finished to help Jim with the tallies.

26. That investigation if one can believe him will redeem our public image.

27. The Commissioner of Internal Revenue during our lengthy talk left no doubt that he intended to curb tax evasion by forceful means.

28. The obvious thing to do Mr. Williams is to compare our lease rates with the actual cost of buying an automobile.

29. John Spiller the man handling our investments vetoed Mr. Carr's proposal.

30. "One good practice" he commented "is to revise your price list periodically."

31. The club members full and comfortable sat back in their chairs to watch the entertainment.

32. The container a rare Chinese vase could not be replaced.

33. Janice understanding my reluctance to leave offered me another cup of coffee.

34. One of the items of course can be written off as a business gift.

35. Mr. Jenssen was irritated because his superior Mr. Johanson requested Miss Parker not Miss Cribari as his secretary.

WORK PROJECT 33

Using the Colon

A. Place colons wherever they are required in the following sentences. Some sentences may not require colon punctuation.

1. The major problems were these an unfavorable trade balance, unused industrial capacity, and unemployment.

2. Mr. Holman suggested a possible legislative solution to rising costs increase the postal rate on first-class mail to five cents and on air mail to eight cents.

3. Listed as factors expected to contribute toward a business expansion in the coming year were larger profit totals and rising personal income.

4. Today the National Industrial Conference Board made the following prediction a $32 billion increase in the gross national product to a rate of $569 billion by the end of the year.

5. The auction will begin at 1 00 p.m.

6. Dear Mr. Burks The proposed tax reform legislation now pending has been designed to give businessmen additional incentives to spend money. May we suggest. . . .

7. You will need three additional items a file cabinet, a typewriter, and a desk.

8. Here is a brief list of supplemental reading books Hawley, *Economic Problems;* Murchison, *Recollections of a Financier;* and Burger, *Boom or Bust?*

9. Several promotions have been announced in the last week Mr. Billings, to sales manager; Mr. Lloyd, to senior art director; Mr. Hanahan, to publicity director.

10. Was the first session of the conference to take place at 8 00 a.m. or 8 00 p.m.?

11. Gentlemen According to our information, steel production will soon reach the highest level in five years. . . .

12. She had only one serious failing as a wife she always fell short, by about ten dollars a month, of making ends meet.

13. Follow these simple directions (1) fold the paper toward you across the dotted line, (2) seal, and (3) mail at once.

14. The former presidents have been Richard Carter and Denison Price.

15. Since retiring, I am unable to rid myself of old habits I unconsciously set the alarm for six o'clock, and I keep setting aside left-over meat for sandwiches.

B. After the colon supply details, an explanation, or a formal quotation consisting of several sentences.

Ex: People on low-calorie diets should avoid three foods:

   peanuts, chocolate, and avocados.

1. Eliza pointed out the only sensible solution of our problem: ....

2. Here is my chief complaint about the delivery system: ....

3. There are two points to consider: ....

4. As tour leader, you must assume two major responsibilities: ....

5. The President made the following statement about the role of the tourist in helping create international good will: ....

C. Supply a main thought that will serve to introduce the material that follows the colon.

Ex: Three fruits are in abundant supply: apples, peaches, and pears.

1. .... :
   cleaning my room, writing letters, and telephoning friends.

2. .... :
   Mr. Smith, Miss Williams, Mrs. Jones, and Mr. Johnson.

3. .... :
   Monday, Wednesday, or Saturday.

4. .... :
   to build new plants and to modernize equipment.

5. .... :
   "It is always difficult to predict the outcome of legislative issues, but certainly Congress will consider tariff legislation, tax reform, medical care for the aged, and retraining of the jobless. These issues will deeply affect the finances of millions of American families."

WORK PROJECT 34

Using the Dash and Parentheses

Insert parentheses or dashes in the following sentences. To add interest, one sentence has been included which calls for a colon.

1. Tariff legislation, tax reform, medical care for the aged, higher postal rates what have these widely dissimilar subjects in common?

2. These prices $30 for topcoats, $10 for sweaters, and $50 for suits are the lowest in five years.

3. Salesmen's expense accounts should be handled in this manner record daily hotel bills, cost of meals, and tips; submit a monthly report of expenses; report on income tax application no more than the total amount accumulated on the twelve monthly reports.

4. Most of the architect's suggested changes see Enclosure 2 can be incorporated at very little additional cost.

5. Someone was it you? told my secretary I had requested three tickets.

6. Please hand me never mind.

7. One thing we can always count on in him is this his persistent cheerfulness.

8. You will find everything you need to make your house more beautiful and more comfortable for example, dacron polyester comforters in pink, white, and green.

9. These names and addresses I will send them to you soon will be valuable in your direct-mail advertising.

10. The Hermes 3000 has many advantages not possessed by the average portable typewriter for instance, its ability to cut stencils.

11. If you see Mr. Sloane he works on the second floor, please give him my regards.

12. The report in question it never reached this office supposedly criticized our system of billing.

13. "One generation passeth away, and another generation cometh; but the earth abideth forever. . . ." *Ecclesiastes*

14. The shipment will be made at the proper planting time in your community for example, in early May to the North and in the middle of April to the Midwest.

15. A cottage in Florida, sizable monthly retirement checks even a trip around the world can be yours with the Livemore Retirement Plan.

16. I told Mr. Burch I would there he is now.

17. A 1961 Cadillac de Ville hardtop coupe for $3110, a 1960 Lincoln Continental sedan for $3665 these are just two examples of the best used-car values in our history!

18. I promised Mary I wouldn't reveal but I can tell you, I suppose.

19. "There is no such thing as an illegitimate child; there are only illegitimate parents." *Blossoms in the Dust*

20. Miss Dudley's typing is I've had better secretaries.

21. Thomas Kegley and Marshall Tilley these two salesmen are usually out front in any national competition.

22. We finally agreed to what we had been hoping for all along a compromise.

23. Mr. Meriwether suggested heaven forbid! that we justify the steep rise in prices by giving trading stamps to our customers.

24. Miss Burke said sarcastically that Mr. Hovick's background of experience he was an all-American football player in 1948 made him an admirable choice as our public relations director.

25. Mr. Hall said, "Why can't we merely explain that we oh, I see what you mean!"

WORK PROJECT 35

The Semicolon and Other Internal Marks

Insert hyphens, semicolons, italics (underlining), brackets, ellipsis marks, and apostrophes as they are required in the following sentences. An occasional comma may also be required.

1. Johnson and Johnsons sales advertisements list merchandise of first class quality.

2. That purplish red sweater will probably fade when it is washed I have had discouraging experiences with such colors.

3. These pamphlets are now ready for door to door distribution when you come by to collect them let me show you the new advertisement we have planned for next months edition of the Readers Digest.

4. My two friends great uncle was the great all American penny pincher he debunked any plan for spending money.

5. In one fourth of the tests the highly concentrated solution turned grayish green.

6. Thirty two copies of the book with his hard to get signature will go on sale at two fifteen.

7. Tentatively the artist has chosen to title his mobile The Danglers.

8. Mrs. Dicksons speech had become affected she said oui and nein instead of yes and no.

9. Gertrude Stein once said that Americans (Americans, mind you!) are the oldest people they have been living in the twentieth century longer than anyone else.

10. Mr. Burns appointment has been set for three thirty therefore you should have the film set up by three fifteen.

11. Please check the sailing time of the Matsonia in the San Francisco Chronicle.

12. At fifteen Maude was hired by the manager of the old Victoria Palace a gaudy edifice formerly standing at the corner of First Street and Garner Avenue to appear in Hamlet as the mad Ophelia. (*Editor's note* = a gaudy edifice . . .)

13. Mr. Barton inflects the word maybe as if it were the word no.

14. The books requested are The Missile Age by Paul Smithers Space and Time by John Seagle and Courtney Delgado and Peaceful Uses of Atomic Energy by Richard Seabright.

15. The archeologist in charge of the excavating said today, "There is now proof that only three temples four are mentioned in the writings of Arodius stood in the ancient city of Mylee." (*Editor's note* = four temples . . .)

16. The archeologist in charge of the excavating said today that "   only three temples stood in the ancient city of Mylee."

17. More than two thirds of the men voted for the ex mayors son in law as the new secretary treasurer.

18. The behavior of the pro American students left us in a predicament not of our own choosing.

19. Miss Searcy could almost qualify as an expert in ready to wear clothing her advice is followed by everyone in the store.

20. If a refrigerator car is unavailable, then you have permission to ship via a ventilated car but wire us collect if you cannot secure one day delivery on either.

21. Are there two rs in the word embarrass?

22. On the eve of the new elections, the premier said, "The work is just beginning   " (Indicate that the quoted sentence continues beyond *beginning*)

23. The musical comedy Highbrows and Lowbrows was on nearly every visitors preferred list.

24. Mr. Hefty shouted angrily and gesticulated wildly his partner took a calmer view.

25. A two thirds majority is stipulated in the rule book.

WORK PROJECT 36

Using Quotation Marks

Place quotation marks where they are required in the following sentences. Capitalize the first word of a quotation which is a complete thought or which serves as a complete thought. Some sentences will require comma punctuation, some will require corrected end punctuation, and some will require other marks used internally.

1. She asked where he was going.

2. He replied I am on my way to Murphy's office.

3. Miss Cain is the secretary Miss Ammerman is the treasurer said the president.

4. When we finally discussed details said Thorpe the transaction looked less feasible.

5. Aunt Agatha said mercy and wrung her apron.

6. Miss Cain is the secretary said the president Miss Ammerman is the treasurer.

7. Miss Cain is the secretary said the president the treasurer is Miss Ammerman.

8. No we told them you may not make the trip alone.

9. Has the conference date been set asked Mr. Nelson.

10. Was it Mr. Netherby who said aren't we living in the twentieth century.

11. *Webster's* defines *mystagogue* as one who inititates or interprets mysteries.

12. This anthology contains my two favorite modern poems, The Love Song of J. Alfred Prufrock and Sweeney among the Nightingales.

13. In a chapter called Monkey Business he facetiously alludes to the James Thurber essay How To Adjust Yourself to Your Work and also to a short story called The Ladder of Success.

14. The drowsy receptionist exclaimed, when I shook her, oh, you startled me.

15. How nice of you to say spend the night at our house.

16. When asked what he did for a living, Mr. Pinson said I dye the joke never failed to get a laugh or a smile.

17. Why she queried must you work late again.

18. As the tall column of boxes began to wobble, the apprentice yelled timber and took refuge in the next aisle.

19. The most interesting chapter of *Pacific Paradise* is Marriage Rites.

20. Who said when do we eat.

21. Mr. Williams shouted you have gone too far.

22. The column I am referring to is called The Question Man and is a daily feature of the *Gazette*.

23. Mr. Bruton inquired where the plant was to be located.

24. Suppose said Mr. King that our offer is rejected. Then where will we be?

25. In her letter she said yes I will support your efforts to change the present policy.

26. He said please keep in mind the president's favorite saying, do it today.

27. The short poem carried the prosaic title Springtime.

28. Birches, Stopping by Woods on a Winter Evening, and The Death of the Hired Man are three of his most enduring poems.

29. We concluded that additional investments were not advisable at that time.

30. Yes the layouts are read said the voice at the other end of the line.

15 NUMBERS

Business writing makes free use of numbers written in figures. The reason is obvious: figures are eye catching, emphatic, and economical of space and time. However, business correspondence is also subject to many of the conventions applying to other types of composition; for that reason many numbers must continue to be spelled out. The generalizations listed in this section are meant to guide, not to govern. Authorities differ on some points, and many companies have their own preferences.

SPELLING OUT NUMBERS

- Spell out a number that begins a sentence. If the number requires more than two words, the sentence should be rewritten so that the number can be written in figures.

> Five glass doors have been installed.
>
> The answers received have totaled 121.   (Instead of: 121 answers . . .)
>
> She could recall only the year 1940.   (Instead of: 1940 was . . .)

- Spell out numbers from one to ten, round numbers which are only approximate, and indefinite sums of money.

> Eight applicants have been interviewed today.
>
> There are nearly a thousand checks to be stamped.
>
> Almost twenty thousand dollars will be required for the project.

- Spell out sessions of Congress and the identifying numbers of military bodies and political divisions.

> Eight laws were passed the first day the Seventy-second Congress convened.
>
> The Fourteenth Battalion was transferred to Alaska.
>
> The appointment rewarded his years of leg-work in the Fourteenth District.

- Spell out the time of day when it is followed by *o'clock* or when it is used in an informal manner.

> At ten o'clock there is a coffee break.
>
> Meet me at Janet's at two-thirty.

- Spell out sums of money in legal documents.

    I promise to pay One Hundred Eight-six Dollars ($186).

- Spell out names of centuries and decades.

    the gay nineties   the anxious thirties   the nineteenth century

- Spell out fractions standing alone.

    We had recovered one third of the loss.

- Spell out a street with a number for a name when the number is ten or below. It is also conventional to write out the number of house number *One*.

    Jean Gray
    108 Second Avenue
    Marysville, Missouri

    Living on the corner allowed her to use the distinctive address One Downey Street.

- Spell out the day of the month when it stands alone or precedes the month.

    John arrived on the twelfth of July to inspect the site.
    (Also allowable: John arrived on the 12th of July . . .)

    Please have dinner with us if you are in town on the tenth.

- When two numbers come together in a meaningful relation, spell out the smaller number and express the larger one in figures:

    three 21-foot boards   27 ten-pound notes   7 one-cent stamps

USING FIGURES FOR NUMBERS

- Use figures for all numbers above ten.

    There were 18 books in the order.

    We have in stock 102 cases of eggs and 55 quarts of milk.

    Today I counted 1,986 automobiles in the parking lot.

- Use figures for all numbers in a connected group within a sentence, even though some of the numbers are below ten.

    The first week, 86 students registered; the second week, 11; the third week, 7.

- Use figures for all numbers in the following:

    Addresses:

    Miss Carruthers lives at 6 Easter Avenue but prefers her mail addressed to 12 Winchester Drive, Bywater 6, Maine.

    Precise age: The junior partner is 26 years old.

    Decimals: 1.087   .04   .5

    Market quotations: AT&T 3s at 87½

    Page numbers and divisions of books: Chapter V, Part 1, begins on page 103.

Note. Roman numerals are used with book chapters.

Percentages: A discount of 10 per cent is standard.

Ratios: a ratio of 3 to 1

Sums of money:

>We have billed you for $112 instead of $116.50.

>An increase in tax collections of $16,787 was reported in the newspaper.

>We offer hundreds of interesting items for just 88 cents.

>Here are typical sale items: toothbrushes, 55¢; plastic soap dishes, 15¢; wash cloths, 35¢.

>Effective today, these will be our new prices on the following: trivets, $.65; glass coffee makers, $4.98; aluminum kettles, small size, $5.45.

Weights, dimensions, capacities, distance, etc.:

>The carcass weighed 230 pounds 14 ounces.

>The tank should hold 200 gallons.

>These envelopes are 4 by 6½ inches.

>The road was 10 miles long.

Fractions with mixed numbers:

>The average reaction time of a good driver is 1½ seconds.

Complete Work Project 37

WORK PROJECT 37

Expressing Numbers

Rewrite any of the following sentences in which there are mistakes in expressing numbers in business writing.

1.   1936 was the year this company merged with Majier and Son.

   ....

2.   The 4 men and 2 women were not hurt when the truck rammed into their Ford.

   ....

3.   Nearly $1000 has been spent on 2 new couches and an upholstered chair.

   ....

4.   At eight p.m. the meeting adjourned.

   ....

5.   Her appointments were set for 6 and 7:15 p.m.

   ....

6.   I agree to pay one thousand fifty dollars in 3 months.

   ....

7.   Many new industries sprang up during the 40s and 50s.

   ....

8.   Can you deliver two twenty-five-inch redwood boards and thirty-five 10-inch pine boards by noon tomorrow?

   ....

   ....

9.   ¾ of the directors were in agreement with the chairman.

   ....

10.   The next shipment should arrive on the 14th, and it will be dispatched promptly to your warehouse at 149 8th Street.

   ....

   ....

11.   We are sorry to inform you that your order for 14 display cabinets (2½ by 6 feet) cannot be filled at this time.

   ....

   ....

12.   Aren't you nearly 21 years old?

   ....

13.   Mr. Curtin discovered a ratio of seven to one each time he conducted the tests.

   ....

14. The book contained eighteen chapters and a total of one hundred eighty-nine pages.

....

15. It is expected that approximately $2,000,000 will be set aside by the 88th Congress.

....

....

16. Henry was a member of the 24 Regiment when it was sent to the Pacific theatre of war during the early 40s.

....

....

17. Chapter VII, Part three, is incorrectly labeled as page one hundred twenty-four.

....

....

18. By error the place mats were marked 45¢ instead of $.69, and the canister sets should have been $1.49 instead of $1 and thirty-nine cents.

....

....

....

19. A commission of fifteen percent is normally figured at the retail price.

....

20. Each bundle weighed exactly 115 pounds ten ounces instead of the estimated 116 pounds 2 ounces.

....

....

16 WORD DIVISION

For an esthetically pleasing effect, a typewritten page should have a reasonably even right margin. To achieve this, words of more than six letters are frequently divided at the end of the line. The division is indicated by a hyphen which follows the part of the word placed at the end of the line.

Many typists divide words more often than necessary. It is more desirable to cater to the convenience of the reader than to strive for a precise right margin. A word should never be divided if to do so will blur its pronunciation in the reader's mind.

The dictionary is the best authority for dividing words into syllables, but the following guides indicate the preferred points of word division.

- Words may be divided only between syllables:

ful-fill		fulfi-ll
sea-side		seas-ide
under-stood	**Not**	unde-rstood
mis-placed		misp-laced

One-syllabled words are never divided:

through		thro-ugh
passed	**Not**	pas-sed
kept		ke-pt

- It is preferable to divide only words of six letters or more so that there will be at least three letters in the part of the word at the end of the line and the part of the word carried over to the following line:

con-tinue	insti-gated
indi-cation	pref-erable

- One- and two-letter syllables should not be separated from the remainder of a word. They do not affect the alignment of the right margin sufficiently to justify themselves:

again		a-gain
into		in-to
before		be-fore
reply	**Not**	re-ply
money		mon-ey
weary		wear-y
casually		casual-ly

- Compound words and hyphenated words are divided between their main parts:

| rowboat | (row-boat) | left-handed | (left-handed) |
| serviceman | (service-man) | open-minded | (open-minded) |

- Double consonants are usually divided, but a double consonant on a root word is divided after the root:

| instil-ling | **But** | pass-ing |
| incur-ring | | bless-ing |

- Divide between two separately sounded vowels that come together:

recre-ation   deline-ation

- A vowel standing alone or pronounced as part of a syllable should be included before the hyphen, but when a word is made up of an English root and a suffix, the vowel is included with the suffix:

Vowel standing alone: hes i tate   (hesi-tate)
                        vis i tor   (visi-tor)

Vowel pronounced as part of a syllable: pos si ble   (possi-ble)
                                          tan gi ble   (tangi-ble)

An English root and a suffix: agree-ably
                                deduct-ible
                                impression-able
                                knowledge-able
                                lov-able
                                receiv-able
                                trad-able

- Do not divide a word that is a contraction:

| couldn't | **Not** ⎰ | could-n't |
| wouldn't | ⎱ | would-n't |

- Do not divide proper names, and if possible do not separate titles, degrees, or initials from the surname:

Tinnemann		⎧ Tinne-mann
John C. Polt		⎪ John C.
		Polt
Mr. Dierks	**Not**	⎨ Mr.
		Dierks
John Harvey, M.D.		⎪ John Harvey,
		⎩ M.D.

- If it is necessary to interrupt an address or a date, separate at the end of a unit. Never separate between the month and the day or the city and the zone number:

1886 Devon Way,   **Or even**   1886 Devon   ⎧ 1886
Boston   Way, Boston   ⎪ Devon Way, Boston
Silver Springs 10,   **Avoid** ⎨ Silver Springs
Colorado   ⎪ 10, Colorado
April 29,   ⎪ April
1929   ⎩ 29, 1929

- Do not separate abbreviations or numbers that should come together:

Y.W.C.A.		Y.W.-
	Not	C.A.
$1397.65		$1397.-
		65

- Avoid awkward divisions that will blur the pronunciation in the reader's mind:

sett-   cur-
lement   able

- Do not divide a word (1) at the ends of more than two successive lines, (2) at the end of the last full line of a paragraph, or (3) at the end of the last line of a page.

- If possible, use no more than three divided words to one typewritten page.

Complete Work Projects 38 and 39

WORK PROJECT 38

Hyphenating Words

A. Assume that each word in the following list occurs at the end of a line. Indicate the proper division by writing in the blank at the right the part of the word that would occur before the hyphen; in the next blank write in the part of the word that would be carried over to the next line. If a word should not be divided, underline it. Whenever you are in doubt about the correct syllabication of a word, look it up in the dictionary.

1. affidavit ....

2. dirty ....

3. only ....

4. request ....

5. laundry ....

6. bandwagon ....

7. old-fashioned ....

8. San Jose 11 ....

9. $1,889.89 ....

10. 136 First Street ....

11. Mr. Fred Clark ....

12. Robert Carsten, Ph.D. ....

13. shouldn't ....

14. Bollinger ....

15. strength ....

16. recommend ....

17. benefited ....

18. sensible ....

19. graduation ....

20. N.O.M.A. ....

B. The syllabication of the following words has been taken from *Webster's 3rd*. Insert a diagonal line to indicate all acceptable end-of-line divisions. Some words, like compensation, may have more than one acceptable division: com/pen/sa/tion. If a word does not have an acceptable division, circle it.

1. re cep tion
2. per fec tion ist
3. re frig er a tor
4. con ten tion
5. op por tune
6. bridge mas ter
7. ac cli ma tize
8. ac com plished
9. leop ard
10. mas cu line
11. drear y
12. news let ter
13. John A. Win ters
14. Vin cent Poole, M.D.
15. a stride
16. clas si cal
17. 14 Stout Street
18. on ly
19. re tain
20. right- hand ed

21. in cur ring
22. class ing
23. Chi ca go 51
24. ra tion
25. trans fu sion
26. trace a ble
27. track less
28. un true
29. sub mit ting
30. re load er
31. pa per hang er
32. mi cro switch
33. fra ter nal
34. eye- catch er
35. Doc tor Parks
36. is n't
37. gum my
38. un ev en
39. lop sid ed
40. e con o mist

WORK PROJECT 39

Correcting Copy

The following memorandum contains errors in word division. Place a check mark (√) after the number of each line that contains an error. Because this is a drill, more than three word divisions may be allowed per page.

MEMORANDUM

From: A. L. Nethers   Date: October 5, 19—

To: P. G. Sommer

Subject: DEVELOPMENT OF RESINA CAPPER DISCS WITH MORE NEARLY
           OPTIMUM CHARACTERISTICS

Reference: Your memo to Mr. Fink dated August 15, 19—

The project to develop and improve Resina capper discs has been

reactivated in order to eliminate the disadvantages of all cur-   1 ....

rently approved discs.

What we are now searching for is a high-friction, resistant, non-   2 ....

marking capping wheel. At the time that the Plastics Develop-   3 ....

ment Group researched capping wheels, about a year ago, we were

very much satisfied with the black Droprine produced by Egger-   4 ....

man & Sons. However, in our attempt to cap our bottles as

tightly as possible, we find there is often an objectionable ten-   5 ....

dency for the black wheel to leave a smudge on the cap. Cor-   6 ....

recting this fault is our concern of the moment.

We are presently working with several large suppliers through-   7 ....

out the country but would most certainly welcome thoughts that

the Plastic Application Group may have on the subject. If you

come across any new information within a month, send it to 135   8 ....

Dartmouth Lane, Boston 4, Massachusetts. After that time I will

be at my usual address.

For your information, we now have a test rig at Omaha for compara-   9 ....

tively evaluating capping discs. We feel that it stimulates line-cap-   10 ....

ping, since we are using a six-spindle surplus Resina capper as

the basis of our equipment.

In conclusion, we might add that nearly all our investigation is

centered around polyurethanes. The only reason we are purs-   11 ....

uing this path with several different suppliers is that we will

eventually arrive at the correct combination of fillers and addi-   12 ....

tives necessary to give us the elastomer characteristics which

we require.

        A. L. N.

pl

cc: Mr. Fink

In the spaces provided below, first list the number of the line which contains an error. Then
supply the correction in the other two spaces.

Ex: 1 ....   currently ....

     ....

     ....

     ....

     ....

     ....

     ....

     ....

17 MATURE SENTENCE STRUCTURE

A well-structured sentence is simply one which efficiently and economically guides the reader so that the main thought stands out in proper perspective. Details and less important ideas are incorporated as naming or modifying units which we call dependent clauses, prepositional phrases, verbal phrases, and appositives. These word groups help us avoid the monotony of short, choppy sentences; they make necessary qualifications and establish logical connections.

Having been conditioned to the basic sentence patterns, the parts of speech, and word groups, you are now ready to demonstrate your grasp of the rudiments of sentence mastery— the discussion with which this book began. As a review, the four word groups are illustrated to show how they can stretch a sentence to hold more thought.

Consider these sentences:

(1) Mr. Adams used to be a broker. (2) He worked on the New York Stock Exchange.
(3) He gives reliable advice on securities.

These three sentences lack vitality because they are ineffective and uneconomical. The main idea is expressed in the third sentence; the first two contain related but less important ideas. By subordinating the first two ideas and relating them to the third, many sophisticated structures are possible. To begin with, a prepositional phrase makes it possible to combine the first two sentences:

1 and 2:   Mr. Adams used to be a broker on the New York Stock Exchange.
     3:   He gives reliable advice on securities.

The first two sentences can now be subordinated to the third one in several ways.

As a dependent clause: *Since he used to be a broker on the New York Stock Exchange,* Mr. Adams gives reliable advice on securities.

As a verbal phrase: *Being a former broker on the New York Stock Exchange,* Mr. Adams gives reliable advice on securities.

Mr. Adams gives reliable advice on securities, *having once been a broker on the New York Stock Exchange.*

As an appositive: Mr. Adams, *a former broker on the New York Stock Exchange,* gives reliable advice on securities.

Nothing really new is introduced in the following work projects. If you run into difficulty, turn back to the appropriate discussions of word groups or their punctuation.

Remember that a word group may itself contain other word groups. A verbal phrase, for instance, may be followed by a dependent clause, as in this sentence: Mary, *wearing the hat which she had just bought,* confronted her husband. *Wearing* is the verbal, the key word, but the entire verbal phrase is *wearing the hat (which she had just bought).* In the following work projects, the important thing is to begin the subordinate thought units with the word group specified.

Here are further examples of word groups which in turn contain other word groups:

Mrs. Crosby, *driving the automobile (which she had purchased) (in Italy),* was serenely indifferent to us in our old Ford.
   (The subordinate idea is expressed in the verbal phrase beginning with the key word *driving;* a dependent clause and a prepositional phrase complement the meaning of the verbal phrase)

This product has been designed *for the man (who already has everything).*
   (The prepositional phrase *for the man* controls the introduction into the sentence of the dependent clause that follows it)

Haunted (by failures) (which he could never admit) (to himself), Hartford finally collapsed.
   (*Haunted* is the key word which controls the introduction into the sentence of the two prepositional phrases and the dependent clause)

Complete Work Projects 40–43

WORK PROJECT 40

Subordinating with Prepositional Phrases

Read through each group of sentences to determine which sentence contains the main idea. Then change the subordinate idea into a prepositional phrase and join it to the main idea. In some cases two subordinate ideas can be reduced to one prepositional phrase with two objects. Insert the prepositional phrase in the most logical, meaningful position. Usually no punctuation is required with a prepositional phrase unless it interrupts the normal word order: Norma, *with her new hairdo*, felt unaccustomedly confident of herself.

Ex: The home office was located in Peoria, Illinois. It was there for five years.

   The home office was located in Peoria, Illinois, for five years.

Mr. Patterson's success was assured in two ways. It was assured by his personality. It was also assured by his experience.

   Mr. Patterson's success was assured by his personality and experience.

1. It was April. The sale of rain gear increased 150 per cent.

   ....

   ....

2. Mr. Parks and Mr. Baroni were in Mexico. They were conducting motivational research.

   ....

   ....

3. Albert was in London. It was so cold and foggy that he could never be entirely comfortable.

   ....

   ....

   ....

4. The farmhouse had many rooms. It also had a large yard. It was an ideal place to rear five children.

   ....

   ....

   ....

5. The audit was conducted by two men. They were from Chicago.

   ....

   ....

6. The new clerk soothed the irritated customer. He had a soft voice. In addition he had a sympathetic attitude.

   ....

   ....

   ....

7. The report had to be ready. An hour's time was allowed.

   ....

8. There were drafts. There was poor visibility. The typists were bothered by these things.

   ....

   ....

9. He arrived in Toronto. He decided to visit the museum there.

   ....

   ....

10. We have contracted to add another wing to the building. We will do so in late spring.

    ....

11. We were annoyed by two things. We disliked the delay and the additional expense.

    ....

12. The cycle would repeat itself. Five days would elapse first.

    ....

13. We could solve the difficulty easily. We could draw lots.

    ....

14. Miss Jenkins found the missing letter. It was in the wastebasket.

    ....

15. We needed help. Mr. Davis could help us.

    ....

    ....

WORK PROJECT 41

Subordinating with Dependent Clauses

Read through each group of sentences to determine which sentence contains the most important idea. Change subordinate ideas into dependent clauses and relate them to the main idea. Every completed answer must have at least one dependent clause, but it is allowable to change an occasional sentence into a prepositional phrase. Whenever possible, join two subordinate ideas by a coordinate conjunction. No punctuation is required with noun clauses. Nonrestrictive adjective clauses are set off by comma punctuation. Adverb clauses coming before the main clause are set off by comma punctuation. Adverb clauses beginning with (1) *though* and *although,* (2) *since* and *as,* and (3) *because* introducing evidence for a statement are set off by comma punctuation even when they come in the normal word order after the main thought.

Ex: Robert was an adaptable employee. He tackled every job enthusiastically. He won a promotion within a year.

> Because he was an adaptable employee and tackled every job enthusiastically, Robert won a promotion within a year.

Luann protested something. She was too tired to walk.

> Luann protested that she was too tired to walk.

Mr. White had a cheerful countenance. He asked us to be seated. Then he would take us into his confidence.

> With a cheerful countenance, Mr. White asked us to be seated before he would take us into his confidence.

1. Miss Vaughn soon realized one thing. She was not interested in her job.

    ....

    ....

2. Three companies were eager to obtain the bid. They submitted very low estimates.

    ....

    ....

    ....

3. Mr. Knolton inquired about the meeting. We were having lunch together. We were in the automat.

    ....

    ....

    ....

4. Andrew bought 50 shares of AT & T. He could barely afford them. He has a low income.

....

....

5. I was temporarily operating the switchboard. I was a relief girl. An important call came through for Mr. Berg.

....

....

....

6. The electronic computer processed the data accurately. It performed for one minute. Then it went amuck.

....

....

....

7. Eventually Mr. Dodge will ask us some questions. What were we delivering? How fast were we driving?

....

....

....

8. Bill Tenney had just grown to like Atlanta. Then he was transferred to Buffalo.

....

....

9. The property is located in Oklahoma. It is no longer profitable. For that reason the stockholders voted to sell it.

....

....

....

10. Grandfather suspected it. Mr. Martin had speculated wildly. Grandfather told me so.

....

....

....

WORK PROJECT 42

Subordinating with Verbal Phrases

Read through each group of sentences to determine which sentence contains the main idea. Then change at least one less important sentence into a verbal phrase and relate it to the main thought. Occasionally you may want to use a prepositional phrase or dependent clause, but each completed answer must contain at least one verbal phrase. Nonrestrictive verbal phrases and shifted verbal phrases are set off by comma punctuation; restrictive verbal phrases are not.

Ex: Mr. Offerman changed his mind. He strode aggressively toward the counter.

      Changing his mind, Mr. Offerman strode agressively toward the counter.

      Mr. Offerman, changing his mind, strode aggressively toward the counter.

There was continual bickering in the family. It threatened their marriage.

      The continual bickering in the family threatened their marriage.

Elizabeth was encouraged by her friends. She was encouraged by her former producer. She decided to do something. She would make a comeback.

      Encouraged by her friends and her former producer, Elizabeth decided to make a comeback.

1. The sound of the alarm frightened the burglar. He hastily left the warehouse.

....

....

2. The money was lying on the table. It bothered the woman. Its mere presence bothered her.

....

....

3. Jane saw the ticket. It was on the floor. She picked it up gleefully.

....

....

4. Mrs. Matthews bought the pin. She wished to give it to her sister.

....

....

5. My husband didn't see the fender. It was damaged in the accident.

....

....

6. Edith was an unhappy child. She was torn between two loyalties.

   ....

   ....

7. The client rose to his feet. He cleared his throat. He handed me the letter nervously.

   ....

   ....

8. They repaired toys for needy children. It was their only hobby.

   ....

   ....

9. Margaret tried to prevent a collision. She honked at the man. He was straddling the center line.

   ....

   ....

10. The employees wanted to end the strike. They called a meeting. They wanted to decide what to do.

    ....

    ....

    ....

11. The two men had missed one opportunity to make their fortunes. They certainly did not intend to miss another.

    ....

    ....

12. I had to determine a means of reducing costs. I requested that a time and motion study be made in the assembling department.

    ....

    ....

    ....

13. *Nation's Business* is the oldest and most widely read publication in the business field. It can attract as writers top level administrators, economists, and researchers.

    ....

    ....

14. California manufacturers have recently produced some unique harvesting machines. They have been designed to cut costs and to reduce the dependency on an uncertain labor supply.

    ....

    ....

    ....

15. He knew every phase of the business. That fact was Mr. Bassett's chief qualification for promotion.

    ....

    ....

WORK PROJECT 43

Subordinating with Appositives

Read through each group of sentences and decide which sentence contains the most important idea. At least one less important sentence should be changed into an appositive to relate to a noun in the main sentence. You may also use prepositional phrases, dependent clauses, and verbal phrases. Remember that a nonrestrictive appositive requires comma punctuation.

Ex: Mr. Murphy retired. His assistant took charge of the office. His name was Mr. Barker.

   After Mr. Murphy retired, his assistant, Mr. Barker, took charge of the office.

The most satisfactory product was Kleen King. It was a detergent. It left no filmy suds.

   The most satisfactory product was Kleen King, a detergent which left no filmy suds.

The Johnsons had only one son. His name is Lyndon. He entered politics at the insistence of his wife. She is a professional clubwoman.

   The Johnsons' son, Lyndon, entered politics at the insistence of his wife, a professional clubwoman.

1.   He arrived on Tuesday. It was the first day of the conference. He arrived minutes before he was scheduled to speak.

   ....

   ....

   ....

2.   We live in the same apartment building with Roger Boris. He is a baseball player. He is making a fine reputation for himself this season.

   ....

   ....

   ....

3.   The personnel manager hired Barbara Hooten. She is a graduate nurse. She is to supervise the innoculations.

   ....

   ....

4.   Mr. Hall has several sons. One is named Jim. He built the motorboat. He built it in his spare time.

   ....

   ....

5. His secretary was an officious woman. She had worked for him for ten years. She handled his public relations.

   ....

   ....

6. Polprene is a tough plastic. Its weather-resistant properties were discovered during the Korean campaign. They were discovered by an army sergeant.

   ....

   ....

   ....

7. Hal March has been hired by Goodman & Sons. That company is a subsidiary of the Arnold Drug Company.

   ....

   ....

8. Frederic Barnes is the president of the company. He is also its chief stockholder. He recommended the merger.

   ....

   ....

9. They spent their vacation at Carmel-by-the-Sea. It is a well-known resort in California. It is less than a few hours' drive from San Francisco.

   ....

   ....

   ....

10. Miss Wheatley is a superb bowler. She gave us a victory. We played against the company executives. We played at the Plaza Recreation Center.

    ....

    ....

    ....

18 WORDS FREQUENTLY CONFUSED

accept—to take willingly
except—to exclude, leave out

To accept the money.
All except one of them.

affect—to influence
effect—to bring about

The medicine affected me adversely.
He effected a change in policy.

all together—the group as a whole
altogether—completely, wholly

The men were singing all together.
We were altogether puzzled.

amount—applied to things in mass
number—applied to things that are counted one by one

A great amount of time, money, energy.
A number of people, minutes, cars.

capital—the city which is a seat of government
capitol—a building that houses the legislature
capital—wealth

A guided tour of the capital.
The right wing of the capitol.
The capital for starting a business.

council—an advisory body
counsel—a legal adviser
counsel—advice
consul—a commerical representative of a foreign nation

The Council on Dental Therapeutics.
Her counsel refused the offer.
You need legal counsel.
The British consul invited us to tea.

compliment—praise
complement—that which completes or harmonizes with

The compliment was certainly deserved.
Blue is the complement of orange.

credible—believable
creditable—worthy of credit

Her explanation was credible.
A creditable performance on opening night.

continual—frequently repeated
continuous—without ceasing

He disliked her continual complaining.
The machine made a continuous noise.

economic—pertaining to the production and distribution of material goods to satisfy human needs
economical—thrifty

The economic condition of an under-developed country.

An economical price for white goods.

eminent—outstanding, distinguished
imminent—pending, ready to occur

An eminent man in the community.
An imminent danger of inflation.

envelop—a verb: to cover
envelope—a noun: a cover for a letter

The fog envelops the house periodically.
You forgot to address the envelope.

famous—well known and approved of
notorious—well known but not approved of

The famous movie star.
The infamous days of the Barbary Coast.

211

farther—preferred for referring to distance
I walked farther than you.

further—preferred for referring to degree
Let's have no further argument.

fewer—describes things that can be counted one at a time
Fewer delays, fewer people.

less—describes things in mass
Less time, less effort, less honesty.

formally—in a prescribed form
We were introduced formally.

formerly—at a previous time
He was formerly the Italian consul.

liable—responsible for
The company is liable for injuries sustained by employees.

likely—probable
It is likely to rain by midnight.

luxuriant—characterized by lush growth
Luxuriant foliage, luxuriant hair.

luxurious—expensive
Luxurious apartment, luxurious furnishings.

material—the stuff from which things are made
The material for the clothes.

materiel—stocks of supplies, equipment, and apparatus as distinguished from personnel
Mr. Hicks wanted an inventory of materiel to accompany the report.

most—an adjective
Most people like chocolate.

almost—an adverb used chiefly in the expression *almost all*
Almost all the tickets were sold.

per cent—by the hundred; used after figures
His sales were 15 per cent higher.

percentage—part of the whole; used without figures
A small percentage of the employees chose to take another week of vacation.

personal—private
This is a personal matter.

personnel—the employees of a firm
Most of the clerical personnel have had college-level training.

practicable—capable of being practised
Strengthening the timbers seems practicable.

practical—realistic, sensible, economical
Displaying goods in a practical manner.

principal—a sum of money
The principal on the loan.

—the head of a school
The principal had to speak to Johnny.

—main or chief
The principal objection is the cost.

principle—a code of behavior
It is not my principle to misadvertise.

respectfully—showing respect or honor
He respectfully stood aside for the old man.

respectively—each in the order given
The box of candy and the corsage are for Miss Blatt and Miss Hodges respectively.

sight—view
There stood a terrible sight!

site—a location for a building
The site for the new factory.

cite—to quote from
He cited a passage from the Bible.

stationary—immovable
A stationary object.

stationery—writing supplies
The stationery with the letterhead.

their—a possessive pronoun
Their suggestion was accepted.

there—an adverb indicating place
Put the file over there.

they're—a contraction: they are
They're not certain.

who's—a contraction: who is
Who's the new jobber?

whose—a possessive pronoun
Whose lunch is this?

your—a possessive pronoun
Your luggage has been sent ahead.

you're—a contraction: you are
You're spilling the coffee.

Complete Work Project 44

WORK PROJECT 44

Avoiding Confused Words

Fill in the correct word in the space provided.

1. accept, except

   to .... an invitation

   all .... one person

   please .... my gratitude

2. economic, economical

   United States .... policy

   an .... automobile

   appeals to ....-minded people

3. amount, number

   a small .... of people

   the .... of energy per gram

   the .... of mistakes made

4. consul, council, counsel

   the British .... in New York City

   the town ....

   the .... for the defense

   follow good ....

5. capital, capitol

   the .... to invest in real estate

   Washington, D.C., the national ....

   plans for remodeling the .... to gain more office space

6. continual, continuous

   a .... cycle of growth in living organisms

   his .... flirtation with danger

   his .... lapses of memory

7. eminent, imminent

   a storm appears ....

   an .... diplomat

   our success appears to be ....

8. site, sight, cite

   to .... the source of the information

   a choice .... for a new school

   the .... of happy faces

   the .... of our future headquarters

9. their, there, they're

   .... approval

   set the basket ....

   .... not altogether to blame

   .... are the missing files

10. compliment, complement

    to be paid a ....

    an insincere ....

    drapes chosen to .... the rest of the room.

11. That is the man (whose, who's) car you damaged. ....

12. It's against the company (principle, principal) to refuse service to anyone. ....

13. Mr. Mahoney discussed the (principle, principal) causes of customer dissatisfaction. ....

14. The trailer and the lift were purchased by Reilly & Son and Springfield Van Lines (respectively, respectfully). ....

15. (Less, Fewer) clerks will be needed in the new branch store. ....

16. How much (farther, further) is it to the shopping center? ....

17. Let us (accept, except) the award for you. ....

18. Is he (likely, liable) to respond to your proposal? ....

19. The (per cent, percentage) of customers using credit cards is still quite small. ....

20. The candidates were greeted (formally, formerly) by the members of the reception committee. ....

21. (Most, Almost) all the pole lamps have been sold. ....

22. Spending so much money to advertise non-perishable items does not seem (practical, practicable). ....

23. The service at the banquet was (all together, altogether) satisfactory.

24. Miss Thompson gave the only (credible, creditable) account of the mishap. ....

25. A competent decorator could give these old waiting rooms a (luxuriant, luxurious) atmosphere. ....

26. The architect derived his effect from the natural color of the building (materiel, material) itself.   ....

27. If you want a (personal, personnel) reaction, ask Dick Bender.   ....

28. The recent recession has (affected, effected) our competitors, too.   ....

29. This shoplifter is (famous, notorious) for the number of traps he has eluded.   ....

30. All the (stationary, stationery) equipment was dismantled and shipped to Delaware when the factory shut down.   ....

31. The new issue of stock was meant to increase the company's working (capital, capitol).   ....

32. The new (envelops, envelopes) have been printed with an attractive return address.   ....

33. The time limitation meant that the committee could not pursue its investigation any (farther, further).   ....

34. The customers had bought up (almost, most) all the sale items before ten o'clock.   ....

35. The (effect, affect) which a bright, appealing package can have on a customer is now firmly established by motivational research.   ....

36. The so-called law of supply and demand is a complex (economical, economic) principle.

37. When completed, Sutro Towers will be a (luxurious, luxuriant) apartment hotel.   ....

38. The current trend toward a bear market is (liable, likely) to continue for some time.   ....

39. (Less, Fewer) important items than usual are on the agenda for the meeting Friday afternoon.   ....

40. The conference chairman was introduced as a man (eminent, imminent) in the field of political science.   ....

19 WORDS AND EXPRESSIONS TO AVOID

If you had some reason for wishing to write a letter of application that would eliminate you from consideration, then you could achieve that result with a generous sprinkling of the words and expressions listed in this section. Although incomplete sentences and incoherent thought are more obvious defects in writing, your apparent inability to discriminate between the conventional and the mistaken would disqualify you for letter writing and executive-level work.

A few of the items reflect carelessness in pronouncing words (could *of* done rather than could *have* done). Some are misspellings of very common words (*alright* instead of *all right*). One is based on a confusion of two separate words (*irregardless* as a blend of *irrespective* and *regardless*). Others are examples of poor diction (*swell, awfully*).

One or more of these words and expressions will occasionally slip into our conversation, but they are not acceptable in routine correspondence. Read through the list carefully. You may find that you have let at least one item carry over into your writing.

alright   A mistaken and unacceptable spelling of *all right*.

and etc   Use *etc.* by itself. The word *and* is already included in the meaning of *etc.* (*and so forth*).

anywheres   A mistaken and unacceptable variation of *anywhere*.

awfully   a colloquial word meaning *very*. It is imprecise and should not be used in business letter writing (The program was *awfully* good). Use *very, extremely, unusually,* or some other more precise adverb.

>   The program was *surprisingly* good.

could of, should of, would of   Because *have* is often clipped in pronunciation to *uv*, some people mistakenly write it as *of* (I *could of* told you so).

>   I *could have* told you so.

got   Mistakenly used to mean *have* (I *got* to go now) or used in addition to *have* (They *have got* to be on time).

>   I *have* to go now. They *have* to be on time.
>
>   **Better:**   I *must* go.   They *must* be on time.

had of   *Of* cannot be used as a helping verb (If I *had of known* you were coming....).

>   If I *had known* you were coming....

had ought to   A wordy and unacceptable way of saying *should* (They *had ought to* get to work).

> They *should* get to work.

in regards to   A mistaken form of *in regard to*. Even the correct form should be avoided, for it is a stereotyped way of saying *about* (I decided to write to you directly *in regard to* the damage).

> I decided to write to you directly *about* the damage.

in back of   A wordy way of saying *behind* (Look *in back of* the desk).

> Look *behind* the desk.

irregardless   A mistaken blending of *irrespective* and *regardless* (The goods have not moved *irregardless* of the reduction in price).

> The goods have not moved *regardless* of the reduction in price.

party   Acceptable only in legal documents (The *party* of the first part agrees to. . . .). Do not substitute it for *person* in ordinary writing (A *party* whom I had not met previously. . . .).

> A *person* whom I had not met previously. . . .

same   A stereotyped and unacceptable substitute for *it* (Your request for information has been received, and *same* has been forwarded to Mr. Barnes).

> Your request for information has been received, and *it* has been forwarded to Mr. Barnes.

try and   An unacceptable substitution for *try to* (Please *try and* stay awake).

> Please *try to* stay awake.

swell   A slang word which does not clearly describe anything (a *swell* man, a *swell* report, a *swell* schedule).

> A *thoughtful* man, an *informative* report, a *convenient* schedule.

Complete Work Project 45

WORK PROJECT 45

Eliminating Objectionable Words and Expressions

Underline any word or expression that would be unacceptable in business letter writing. In the blank at the right, fill in the acceptable word or expression. Some sentences are correct; place a C in the blank after them.

1. He wants the convertible irregardless of the expense. ....

2. Miss Jones is a swell stenographer. ....

3. The party who just telephoned you is a man. ....

4. Try and interview the vice president in charge of sales. ....

5. You should of seen the expression on my wife's face! ....

6. Look who is standing in back of you! ....

7. I want to talk to you in regards to your inspection. ....

8. The defective mechanism arrived yesterday, and same has now been repaired. ....

9. Mr. Perkins had ought to know better. ....

10. You got to cross-file these papers, Miss Dow. ....

11. Mr. Higgins' comments were awfully perceptive. ....

12. I can't locate Mr. Burton anywheres. ....

13. These handles are available in many lightweight materials: aluminum, plastic, rubber, and etc. ....

14. It will be alright for you to tour the factory. ....

15. The workmen were upset in regard to the delay. ....

16. If the customer had of saved his receipt, we could honor his claim. ....

17. With that information we could of made a killing on the current bear market. ....

18. The display must be finished regardless of the overtime expense. ....

19. The sale should have been more widely advertised. ....

20. Several parties have responded to the questionnaire. ....

20 STYLES OF BUSINESS LETTERS

Typically a business letter consists of the following parts:

1. a printed letterhead or return address (and date)
2. an inside address
3. a salutation
4. the body of the letter
5. a complimentary close
6. the company name
7. a handwritten signature followed by the same name typewritten (and frequently a title or department)
8. identifying initials
9. enclosure notes and/or the distribution of carbon copies

The arrangement of these lines on the page is referred to as letter style. Though individual companies or employers may sometimes impose slight modifications, there are four basic styles, and only two of these are commonly used. The opening and closing lines of a letter are punctuated in an open, closed, or standard manner.

The main purpose of a business letter is to convey a communication with simplicity and directness. It relies on clear, everyday English to state its purpose in a courteous manner. It does not require any special formulas; in fact, the modern tendency is to avoid cliches such as *We beg to inform you* or *Thanking you in advance*. Both its form and content are designed to help the reader abstract from it what he needs as rapidly as possible.

A good business letter begins to make an impression from the moment it is unfolded. If it is neatly and accurately typed, if its various parts are balanced on the page for a pleasing effect, then it invites careful reading.

A business letter does not require ornamentation. It is enough if the stationery is of good quality, if it is embellished with a modest letterhead, and if the words are evenly typed on a good ribbon.

INDENTED STYLE; CLOSED PUNCTUATION

Both indented style and closed punctuation are rarely used today. This model has been included as a comparison for understanding the other models.

                                        14 Vermont Avenue,
                                          Kansas City 11, Missouri,
                                            August 19, 19—.

Humboldt Metals,
    546 Baker Street,
        Marcus, Ohio.

Gentlemen:

        ....
    ....
    ....

        ....
    ....
    ....
    ....

        ....
    ....

                                        Very truly yours,

                                        Martin C. Jones

                                        Martin C. Jones

BLOCK STYLE; OPEN PUNCTUATION

In this style all the parts of the letter begin flush with the left margin. Open punctuation means that no punctuation is used after the opening or closing lines except for abbreviations. This style is the most economical one for the typist, yet some people find it objectionable because it overweights the left side of the letter.

SWIFT ASSOCIATES

1447 Tenth Street • Orlando, Florida • Tel: 135-1862

October 1, 19—

Mr. Russell Anson, Jr.
Burton Office Equipment Co.
27 Maple Street
Albany, Georgia

Dear Mr. Anson

....

....

....

....

....

....

....

....

Yours very truly

SWIFT ASSOCIATES

Harold B. Hill

Harold B. Hill
Controller

HBH: ce
Enclosure

MODIFIED BLOCK STYLE; STANDARD PUNCTUATION

This model is second in popularity. The return address (if there is no printed letterhead) and date are on the right-hand side, as are the complimentary close, the company name, and the signature. In the standard system of punctuation, no punctuation is used outside the body of the letter except after the salutation and complimentary close and after abbreviations.

SWIFT ASSOCIATES

1447 Tenth Street • Orlando, Florida • Tel: 135-1862

October 1, 19—

Mr. Russell Anson, Jr.
Burton Office Equipment Co.
27 Maple Street
Albany, Georgia

Dear Mr. Anson:

....

....

....

....

....

....

....

....

                                 Yours very truly,

                                 SWIFT ASSOCIATES

                                 Harold B. Hill

                                 Harold B. Hill
                                 Controller

HBH: ce
Enclosure

MODIFIED BLOCK STYLE WITH INDENTED PARAGRAPHS; STANDARD PUNCTUATION

This model is undoubtedly the most popular and the one all business people should be acquainted with. This model is exactly like the preceding one except that the first line of each paragraph is indented five spaces to the right.

SWIFT ASSOCIATES

1447 Tenth Street • Orlando, Florida • Tel: 135-1862

October 1, 19—

Mr. Russell Anson, Jr.
Burton Office Equipment Co.
27 Maple Street
Albany, Georgia

Dear Mr. Anson:

....

....

....

....

....

....

....

....

                                                 Yours very truly,

                                                 SWIFT ASSOCIATES

                                                 Harold B. Hill

                                                 Harold B. Hill
                                                 Controller

HBH: ce
Enclosure

ATTENTION AND SUBJECT LINES

Attention and subject lines are often used as time-savers. The attention line directs the letter to the person in a company most likely to be concerned by it or to take action on it, and the subject line immediately lets the recipient know what the letter is about. A letter may have only an attention line or a subject line, or it may contain both.

Block Style

Judson Steel Company
906 Market Street
Oakland 5, California

Attention: Mr. Walter Cartwright

Gentlemen:

PROPOSED MERGER WITH
YUBA ERECTORS

Modified Block

Judson Steel Company
906 Market Street
Oakland 5, California

Attention: Mr. Walter Cartwright

Gentlemen:

PROPOSED MERGER WITH
YUBA ERECTORS

THE SECOND PAGE

When a letter continues beyond one page, the name of the addressee, the page number, and the date of the letter are placed one inch from the top of the following page. The body of the letter is then continued three spaces below the identifying information.

Mr. Gunter Scheller   Page 2   May 17, 19—

....

....

Mr. Gunter Scheller

Page 2

May 17, 19—

....

....

THE INTER-OFFICE MEMORANDUM

Nearly every firm that is divided into departments or contains branch offices makes use of a special letter form known as the inter-office memorandum. It is a time-saver and involves no special problems of style or punctuation.

MEMORANDUM

To: P. N. Hooker   Date: May 11, 19—

From: P. T. Hardman

Subject: Revising the Production Schedule

Reference: Your memorandum to Mr. Rogers dated April 10

....

....

....

....

....

....

                                                                        P. T. H.

lb

21 COMMON BUSINESS TERMS

There are as many specialized business vocabularies as there are businesses and services. A complete list would be a convenience but not a necessity. On your first job you will quickly absorb the terms peculiar to your line of work. As a secretary or clerk in an insurance company, for instance, you could hardly get through the first day without running into *decedent, premium, deduction clause,* and *mutual company.* Within a few weeks these terms would take on a meaning exceeding any dictionary definitions.

The terms in this section are an attempt to cut across specialized areas and select those that most business men and women might reasonably be expected to share. The assumption is that nearly every business concern will have a typical organization (management, personnel, production, accounting, etc.). It is also assumed that correspondence of some kind is required and that at some time or other most of us are involved with transportation, communication, shipping, mailing, merchandising, business law, and finance. We also share a belief in the same economic system.

Word mastery consists of four things: recognizing a word, pronouncing it, spelling it, and using it meaningfully in context. Men who came up in business "the hard way" (without benefit of much formal education) used to attribute a good deal of their success to word building. Often they were quoted as saying they spent half an hour a day reading a dictionary or memorizing lists of words. That may be true, but the formula was probably their sensitivity to words and how others used them. At any rate, your best use of the dictionary is to use it after you have discovered a need to learn or use a word.

Be extremely observant of the sentence in which a word is discovered, for the dictionary definition of a word does not always prepare you to use it. A student might look up *gamut* and see the one-word synonym *range.* He might then mistakenly write, "The cattle have overgrazed the gamut." But if he recalls the context in which he discovered the word, he can not only choose the proper definition but also, in turn, use the word correctly. The original sentence "The shades and tints of these new cotton fabrics run the gamut of the color charts" might lead to "His stories about himself as a student ran the gamut of human hardship."

The terms in this section have been worked into the exercises throughout the rest of the book to give you familiarity with them.

accountant   One who sets up, maintains, or adjusts the financial operation of a business.

   Mr. Hawkins directed the head accountant to prepare a new financial statement.

acid test   A calculation designed to test the ability of a business to pay its debts quickly. If a business can show a favorable ratio of liquid assets to liabilities, it is considered a good credit risk.

> Our source of information doubted that the Johnson-Whitcombe Laboratories could pass the acid test.

adjudication   The decision a court makes in determining an issue or a dispute.

> Because of the unfavorable adjudication, the company is forced to change its retirement policy.

affidavit   A statement in writing which is signed and sworn to before an authorized person, usually a notary.

> Under that law, officials had to sign affidavits each year that they were not members of the Communist Party.

affluent society   A term coined by the American economist J. K. Galbraith and applied to a society in which there is a superabundance of material goods available to all its members.

> In an affluent society like ours, it is frequently the function of advertising to create a demand for goods which we neither need nor desire.

agenda   A schedule of the business to be considered at a formal meeting.

> My secretary is preparing the agenda for the meeting at four o'clock.

amalgamation   The combining of two or more corporations to form a larger one.

> The stockholders generally favor the proposed amalgamation with Coinway Inc.

amortization   The process of removing a debt by a series of periodic payments to a sinking fund, a creditor, or an account.

> "Amortization of the loan," I explained to her, "meant that the interest on the unpaid balance would decrease with each subsequent payment on the principal."

annuity   An amount of money payable yearly. Usually it is the return from an investment made years earlier and designed to give a person a retirement income.

> The annuities were arranged to begin one month after her husband's retirement.

arbitration   A method of settling a dispute between labor and management by using a third party to decide the differences between them. The government often acts as the third party.

> Two Washington officials arrived today to help in the arbitration involving the Teamsters Union and the Matson Co.

assets   The real property, machinery, cash, and other resources of a person or business.

> At the end of the fiscal year, Hardman Research Corporation listed assets in excess of one million dollars.

audit   An examination of the financial condition of a business by a person or company authorized to verify and certify the correctness of the records.

> Our ledgers will be sent to the downtown office for the annual audit.

automation   A highly controlled process of manufacturing or servicing which is operated automatically by electronic devices and reduces human labor to a minimum.

> Automation speeds up production and reduces labor costs.

balance of payments   A summary of the international transactions of a country or region over a period of time including commodity and service transactions and gold movements.

The total balance of payments of the United States is calculated with respect to the rest of the world, not to merely one country.

balance of trade   The difference in value between a country's exports and imports.

The President's advisor maintains that high tariffs are not the best means of maintaining a satisfactory balance of trade with foreign countries.

bear market   A condition of the market when stock prices in general decline over an extended period of time.

Mr. Hargreaves carefully hoarded his money, waiting for the next bear market.

boycott   The practice of influencing people not to trade with a particular business firm or buy a particular product; it is used as a means of expressing disapproval.

The boycott against Jones & Son was lifted as soon as the obnoxious three-story sign was removed.

brochure   A small pamphlet used in advertising or selling.

Our brochure describes the advantages of this new blender.

broker or stockbroker   A person who acts as an agent for others in buying and selling merchandise or securities. He normally receives a commission for his service.

Mrs. Dawson had little confidence in her husband's broker.

bull market   A condition of the market when stock prices in general increase over an extended period of time.

Mr. Hargreaves hoped to buy in a bear market and sell in a bull market.

capital   (1)   The total money or property owned by an individual or corporation.
(2)   The total assets of a business in excess of the liabilities.

According to the financial page, East Bay Rentals has increased its capital by $105,000.

capital stock   The total shares of ownership in a corporation.

Though he does not have a recent figure available, Mr. Evans estimates the capital stock at nearly two million dollars.

capitalism   A competitive economic system in which the individual is reasonably free to manufacture and sell goods as he sees fit in order to gain profit. Governmental interference is largely held to protecting the public welfare.

Most of us agreed with him that individual efficiency is at the base of capitalism and the entire free-enterprise system.

carrying charge   A small charge made to an account to carry the cost of keeping records. It is added to the cost of goods purchased on the installment plan.

The carrying charge on the refrigerator we bought is about the same as interest would have been on a loan for a comparable amount.

cartel   An international association of industrial firms for the purpose of regulating production or prices in a particular field.

The government charged that the electronics corporation was a member of a cartel that was forcing abnormally high prices in certain areas of military spending.

cash-and-carry   Sales of merchandise for which the buyer pays cash and takes the product with him.

The new store will operate on a cash-and-carry basis.

channels of distribution   The course taken by the title to goods from the point of production (manufacturers), through agencies (brokers), to the point of consumption (retailers).

> The complexity of hidden taxes can be seen readily by tracing a luxury item through its channels of distribution.

check-off   A convenience whereby an employee's union dues, fees, or special assessments are deducted from his pay and turned over to the union.

> The petition asked that union fees be handled by check-off.

clientele   The body of clients of a professional man or a business.

> Mary Van Droos hopes that her dress shop will attract an exclusive clientele.

closed shop   A business or manufacturing establishment where all the employees must be union members.

> The management and the union officials were deadlocked over the issue of the closed shop.

collective bargaining   A relation between an employer and an employee organization, usually a union, which calls for negotiating agreements about wages and working conditions.

> Teachers in the New York City system now have the right of collective bargaining.

comparative advantage   The difference in the cost of services or goods provided by rival firms. The one which offers the lower price has the comparative advantage. In *comparative shopping*, an employee of one firm "shops" in a rival firm in order to compare prices.

> In eight of ten items checked, Ewell Sundries held the comparative advantage.

competition   The rivalry existing among independent companies. Each company tries to obtain business by offering more attractive goods or more favorable prices than its competitors.

> The competition is so keen in some districts that it has resulted in a price war.

commission merchant   A person who, in return for a commission, completely handles the merchandising of such products as dry goods, fruits, vegetables, grains, and livestock.

> With his years of experience in Iowa as a commission merchant, Uncle Walter could look at a hog and judge its weight within six ounces.

conditional sale   A sale on which the buyer places a down payment and promises to pay the balance on regular installments. The seller may reclaim the merchandise if the buyer discontinues payments.

> Because he failed to keep up the payments and ignored the notices, Mr. Thorton's refrigerator was reclaimed under the terms of a conditional sale contract.

consideration   Something of value put up to make a promise legally binding.

> For a consideration of $500 we will repair the east wall of the garage at Hummel's Furniture Store.

consign   To forward goods to another for the purpose of their future sale.

> Ten gross of these new clocks have been consigned to each of our local retailers.

consolidation   The unification of two or more companies into one.

> Today many big corporations are the result of consolidations and mergers of separate companies.

contract   A legal agreement to do or to refrain from doing something.

> Under the terms of the contract with Motion Picture Purchasing Inc., we are restrained from showing double bills.

controller   Usually the head accountant in a large corporation. He is responsible for supervising the firm's internal financial matters.

The controller is preparing a budgetary estimate for the coming year.

convenience goods   Readily available goods, such as tobacco and magazines, that customers can be expected to buy at frequent intervals.

The site at Locust and Fifth Street is ideal for a small shop specializing in convenience goods.

cooperative   An organization for buying and selling which allows the members some form of discount or profit-sharing. Frequently abbreviated to *coop, co-op.*

Some consumer cooperatives have expanded to the point that they now resemble large shopping centers.

corporation   An association of stockholders with legal authority to operate a business under a specific name. It acts as a single person in owning property, entering into contracts, or borrowing money, and it can be sued. Its powers and liabilities are distinct from those of the separate stockholders.

The president of the new corporation will most likely be its chief stockholder, Cyrus Maginn.

cost-plus   A means of setting the price of manufacture so that there is an agreed-on profit over and above the cost of producing an item.

During World War II, a great number of government contracts were let on a cost-plus basis.

cycle billing   A method of billing retail customers which spreads the work evenly through the month. Customers are billed and sent statements alphabetically beginning with the A's at the first of the month.

At first there were protests from customers who did not understand how it worked, but otherwise we switched over to cycle billing very smoothly.

data processing   An electronic system of handling data through the medium of punched tape. This system of processing avoids repetitive handling and displaces human labor.

A new course in data processing is now being prepared at the city college.

debit   The left-hand side of a ledger account which records debt, or the entry made thereon.

The error was a small item which should have been listed as a debit.

deed   An instrument in writing, signed and sealed, which indicates the ownership of real property.

Mrs. Marple is to bring with her the deed to the property on Elm Street.

deficit   A shortage of funds, especially when income is less than expenses.

Even after operating at a deficit for three months, the company could report a substantial capital gain at the end of the fiscal year.

deficit financing   The action of the government, in times of war or depression, in borrowing money to pay its debts and obligations.

Deficit financing during a depression seldom gives rise to inflation until the final stages of recovery.

demurrage   A charge made for freight shipments which have not been unloaded from the railroad cars within two days after arrival.

According to Mr. Scott, the demurrage on the last shipment seems unaccountably high.

depreciation   A deductible expense in figuring income tax returns. It covers the decrease in value of fixed assets such as tools and equipment and buildings through aging and damage.

> We figure our depreciation on a ten-year basis.

depth interview   An interview that goes beyond the surface details of age, interests, and experience in an attempt to get at the essential personality or capabilities of an applicant. Typically the interviewer poses theoretical problems which the interviewee is asked to solve or comment on.

> Each of the three men has been asked to make an appointment with the personnel manager so that he can conduct a depth interview.

discount   The amount deducted from the list price of an item. A *discount house* is a store where all the merchandise listed is sold at a reduced rate.

> We can offer you a special discount of 5 per cent on large orders.

drop shipper   A wholesaler who does not handle merchandise directly; he solicits orders from retailers, but the merchandise is sent directly from the manufacturer to the retailer.

> Mr. Sothern acts as a drop shipper only because he has no warehouse facilities.

economics   The production, distribution, and consumption of commodities or a significant aspect of it.

> Mr. Worthington will set up the standards by which the economics of electric vs. manual typewriters can be evaluated.

elastic demand   A greater volume of buying that is expected from the public when merchandise is sold at a lower unit price.

> Surprisingly there seems to be no elastic demand for these handy little gadgets.

embargo   A governmental order, usually invoked only in emergencies, which forbids the entry of ships or goods into this country.

> Congress considered placing a temporary embargo on Cuban sugar.

eminent domain   A right which the government can exercise to obtain private property for public use.

> The government acquired the land for the airfield by exercising the right of eminent domain.

entrepreneur   A businessman who owns, promotes, and operates his own enterprise. Loosely speaking, a clever businessman who assumes a great deal of risk.

> Henry Ford, it has been said, was the American entrepreneur who did more than anyone else to establish the pattern of mass production.

equity   The real interest on a piece of property over and above the liens or charges against it. In a sense, the amount of money already paid on a piece of property.

> The Harrisons used the equity in their former home to make the down payment on the new one.

escalator clause   A provision, under a labor-management contract, which ties wage rates to an increase or decrease in the cost of living.

> The revised agreement contains a wage escalator clause.

escrow (in escrow)   A written agreement such as a deed or contract which is turned over to a third party and held until some stipulated condition is fulfilled.

> The deed to the Williamson property is still in escrow.

featherbedding   Providing generously for oneself, often with the implication of disregarding the welfare of others.

The demand that four men work on a job which two could easily handle was called featherbedding by the company representative.

fiscal Of or pertaining to money or money matters.

The fiscal year can coincide with the calendar year or it can begin on any day of the year and end on the same day of the following year.

fixed cost A cost that does not fluctuate with the volume of business being done.

The building rental is our main fixed cost.

franchise Permission granted to a retailer to sell the goods of the manufacturer.

Mr. Spalding has relinquished his franchise with the Hanover Manufacturing Company.

good will The reputation which a reliable company establishes with the public by fair dealings or quality merchandise or efficient service.

The telephone company's determination to institute all-digit dialing has not created good will.

grievance A complaint or feeling of injustice which workers direct toward management or ownership.

In addition to the reduction of wages, the workers had other grievances against the railroads in those early years.

gross national product The money value of the total goods and services produced during the year.

The gross national product has been increasing annually since the end of the war.

impulse goods Goods which customers buy on impulse (rather than by plan) because of an exceptionally appealing display.

Women respond more readily than men to impulse goods, but men buy more expensive things when their fancy is taken.

inflation A period of rapid rise in prices and wages as a result of an oversupply of money and credit and an undersupply of goods and services to be purchased. *Spiraling inflation* denotes an extended period of increasing inflation in which increased prices lead to increased salaries lead to increased prices without a leveling off.

The President's appeal to the steel companies not to increase the price of steel was a move to forestall further inflation.

itinerary A detailed schedule of a trip including the times of arrival and departure.

Mr. Winters is including in his itinerary a brief tour of the metallurgical laboratory at Duluth.

jobber A middleman who buys goods in large quantities from wholesalers or producers or importers and sells them to dealers.

None of the local jobbers were able to supply us with the kind of containers we needed.

laissez-faire The "hands off" theory of letting business operate without governmental interference.

I wonder how many people who claim to believe in laissez-faire are aware of the many benefits that accrue to them from time to time as a result of limited government control?

liability Any debt that is owed by an individual or enterprise.

His liability would probably not exceed six thousand dollars.

lien   A charge upon real or personal property as security for a debt.

> An unpaid tax on real property is a lien that takes priority over any other liens.

liquidation   The process of converting assets into cash, especially when closing a business.

> The liquidation of Mills Brothers has freed a sizable amount of our capital for reinvestment.

liquidity preference   A preference for investments that can be converted into cash quickly. A savings account is one such investment.

> The broker was instructed to mark the order "liquidity preference."

lockout   An employer's action in shutting down a plant as a protest against some demand of his employees which he feels is unfair or unwarranted.

> The recent lockout at Meriwether & Campbell has had economic repercussions in the local retail stores: business is off 50 per cent.

margin   An amount of money representing the difference between the amount a broker will lend against collateral and the market price of the stock. The purchaser deposits this sum with the broker.

> Yesterday the Federal Reserve Board lowered the margin required for purchasing stock.

markdown   A reduction in the original selling price of an item.

> At this morning's conference it was suggested that we try a 10 per cent markdown on all slow-moving goods.

markup   The difference between the cost price of an item and its selling price. Roughly speaking, the profit anticipated on an item.

> These various pieces of costume jewelry have a markup of 50 cents each.

market research   An investigation or study of the social status and income level of a community in order to determine which goods or services are best suited to it.

> Surprisingly, recent market research seems to indicate that people in low to moderate income groups are seldom the purchasers of compact, low-priced cars.

mediation   An arrangement whereby a third person tries to settle the differences between two disputing parties by finding a suitable compromise.

> The mediation was expertly handled by Mr. Brown's new assistant, Mr. Hotchkiss.

merchandising   The buying, selling, and advertising of goods; carrying on a trade.

> Plastic packaging has enormously improved the merchandising of variety store items.

merger   The absorption of one corporation by another existing corporation. The absorbing corporation takes over the franchises, rights, privileges, and properties of the absorbed company.

> The president of Delta Homecraft Tools announced today that the stockholders have voted a merger with Haven Machinery and Supply Co.

monopoly   The exclusive control of the raw materials, production, or distribution of a certain commodity. Generally a monopoly is considered an abuse of the free-enterprise system.

> The government charged that the four men had plotted to bring about a monopoly in the sale and distribution of the new drug.

mortgage   A lien on property, used as security in securing a loan. An additional loan on the same property would be called a second mortgage.

> Aunt Harriet was forced to take a second mortgage on her property in Oroville.

motivational research   A scientific study of the psychological factors that influence consumer buying. Advertisers capitalize on the findings by modifying their presentation of products to assure maximum sales.

> Before he gives us the go-ahead, Mr. Walters would like to see the conclusion drawn from our earlier motivational research in cosmetics.

national debt   The total money owed by the United States Government.

> Almost every Congressman has his own suggestion for decreasing the national debt.

negotiable   The ability to transfer a form, such as a promissory note, from one person to another.

> Your I.O.U. is not negotiable, Mr. Barnes.

net cost   The cost of an item exclusive of the expenses of doing business.

> The net cost of each electric toaster is $15.47.

net income   The actual amount of money one receives on a paycheck after deductions.

> The raise in pay has not meant a significant increase in their net income.

net loss   The unfavorable difference between income and expenses.

> This year the company had a net loss of only $37,500, a slight improvement over last year.

net profit   The favorable difference between income and expenses.

> Fastite Expansion Shells reported a net profit of $36,700 over a six-month period.

net sales   The total or gross sales minus returns and allowances.

> The net sales in the Appliances Department have improved considerably since the extensive remodeling of that area.

net worth   The actual value of the ownership of a business; the favorable difference between the assets and the liabilities.

> Mr. Hardesty reported the net worth of Hardesty Wood Products Co. to be approximately $2 million.

night letter   A relatively inexpensive telegram sent at night when there is less traffic. The minimum charge is based on 50 words, with added charges for each additional group of five words or less.

> Mr. Blicker said to send the message as a night letter if it ran over 40 words.

obsolescence   The enforced retirement or disposition of an asset, such as machinery, before it has served its normally useful life. The loss may occur as a result of new inventions, expansion of facilities, or other economic factors.

> The obsolescence of the boiler in the cannery room will be written off as a legitimate tax deduction.

overhead   The total of the operating expenses in conducting a business enterprise. Wages, insurance, utilities, and stationery are typical expenses figured in the overhead.

> Unless we can cut down our overhead, we will soon be unable to meet competition.

parity price   A price which maintains a constant ratio to another price or group of prices.

> Parity prices are designed to give farmers sufficient money for their produce to buy the things they need.

par value   On stock, the fixed value of each share as set forth in the charter and printed on each stock certificate issued.

    The bidding price for AT&T is now well beyond the par value.

patronage dividend   The yield returned to a member of a cooperative; it is proportionate to the amount of money he has spent on purchases over a specified period of time.

    The patronage dividend can be applied toward further shares of stock in the co-op.

per capita   By individuals or by the individual average.

    The per capita consumption of milk and milk products has increased again this year.

prospectus   A notice about a security which a broker uses to interest investors. It must be approved by the Securities and Exchange Commission.

    The new prospectus for the Birtcher Corporation stock has tempted me to buy more shares soon.

recession   In the business cycle, a recession generally follows a period of marked prosperity. It is characterized by a decrease in wages and buying and an increase in unemployment. It often mirrors a temporary fluctuation of the market.

    The current recession will not force us to postpone the plan to reorganize the production department.

reconciliation   Comparing the balance reported on a bank statement with the last check stub corresponding to the same period of time. If there is a disagreement, it is then necessary to take into account the checks not yet cashed, service charges, or deposits recently made. If the figures still do not correspond, there is probably an error in the figuring of either the bank or the person holding the account.

    On an average the reconciliation of a bank statement should take less than five minutes.

seal   The impression made in the lower left corner of a written instrument to confirm that it is legal.

    The contract, signed and under seal, will be delivered to your office by special messenger tomorrow morning.

seniority   The length of time an employee has been with a firm. It is often a consideration when a promotion is being considered or when a layoff threatens. An employee with fifteen years of service would have seniority over one with only ten years.

    Mr. Boyer had more seniority, but Mr. Zenor was the only employee with an engineering degree.

shopping center   A concentration of carefully laid out stores in a suburban area. It may consist of one building or a group of related structures with access to adequate parking facilities. Usually a family can do most of its daily shopping in such a center. Typically there will be a supermarket, jewelry store, clothing store, variety store, hardware, barber shop, beauty shop, etc.

    The new shopping center planned for the Mountain View development will have parking space for three thousand vehicles.

sinking fund   Money which is periodically set aside to pay off a debt or build up a fund for some specific purpose.

    The money already paid into the sinking fund amounts to nearly thirty thousand dollars.

solvent   Having the ability to pay all one's legal debts.

This company has not been solvent for three consecutive years.

specialty shop   A store that specializes in one type of merchandise, such as candy.

The new commercial building on Blue Ridge Boulevard will have six units suitable for specialty shops.

speculation   Buying stocks or entering a business with the hope of making a large profit in a short period of time.

As a means of curtailing speculation, the federal income tax places a penalty on stocks sold before the owner has held them for six months.

stockholder   A person who owns stock in a corporation. His liability is conditioned by the amount he has invested.

Thirty-three stockholders were present at the meeting; the forty-seven others appointed Ralph Burns to vote for them.

subsidiary company   A company owned and controlled by a larger company known as a holding company.

One of our subsidiary companies, Comstock Mining, has requested permission to study our system for attracting qualified geologists.

subsidy   A payment which the government makes in order to control the law of supply and demand. Farmers, for instance, are often paid not to raise crops which are already in oversupply.

Any proposed new subsidies on cereal grains will meet with resistance on the floor of Congress.

tariff   A tax which the government collects on certain imported merchandise.

Putting up a high tariff wall not only stops foreign imports but tends to limit United States exports as well, for foreign countries need the money derived from trade to buy from us.

tickler or tickler file   A file which serves as a reminder. It is usually set up according to dates.

A notation about the substitution was placed in the sales tickler for June 10.

time and motion study   An analysis of a particular job in order to see if it can be accomplished more efficiently. Each part of the task is measured according to the minutes involved and the kind and number of body movements required of the worker.

Mr. Stone has lent me his secretary for the time and motion study in the personnel office.

trade association   An organization of businesses manufacturing or producing merchandise of the same nature. It serves as a clearinghouse of useful information.

Among the trade associations the reaction to the new tariff proposals has been mixed.

vendor   One who sells merchandise.

Street vendors have almost disappeared from the American scene.

vested interest   Interest in a business transaction generated by financial or family ties.

Richard has a vested interest in seeing to it that Mandeville-Jacobsen gets that soft-drink advertising account.

voucher   Evidence that the money has been paid in a business transaction. A canceled check or a receipt is the usual voucher.

If you will refer to our Voucher #166-23, you will see that 10 gross of embossed napkins were included in your last order.

warranty   A pledge that an item of merchandise is safe or genuine. An *implied warranty* is imposed by law; an *expressed warranty* can be oral but is usually stated in writing.

According to the warranty, the agent for this coffee maker is authorized to replace any defective model within six months of purchase.

wholesaler   A middleman. He buys merchandise in large quantities and then resells and distributes them to retailers.

The wholesaler quoted us a discount rate of 5 per cent on broken lots.

Complete Work Projects 46-50

WORK PROJECT 46

Mastering Business Terms:
Accountant to Carrying Charge

A.   In the blank at the right fill in with the word in parentheses which is best defined by the explanation or description.

1.   an examination of the financial records
     (audit, annuity, adjudication)   ....

2.   paying off a debt by systematic payments
     (amortization, balance of payments, arbitration)   ....

3.   yearly income from an investment made years earlier
     (assets, capital, annuity)   ....

4.   a condition of the stock market when it is desirable to sell   ....
     (bull market, bear market, affluent society)

5.   a third party who decides a dispute
     (agent, arbitrator, accountant)   ....

6.   a means of determining whether or not to extend credit to
     a company
     (amalgamation, automation, acid test)   ....

7.   the total shares of stock in a corporation
     (annuities, capital stock, assets)   ....

8.   the difference in value between exports and imports
     (bull market, balance of trade, balance of payments)   ....

9.   a list of the business to be transacted at a meeting
     (agenda, affidavit, amalgamation)   ....

10. the joining of two or more corporations into one large one   ....
     (amalgamation, adjudication, amortization)

B.   Incorporate each term into a sentence of your own composing. Refer to the glossary for an illustration, but imitate the sentence you find there—do not merely copy it.

1.   affluent society   ....

....

....

2.   capitalism   ....

....

....

3.   boycott   ....

....

....

4. brochure ....

....

....

5. automation ....

....

....

6. arbitration ....

....

....

7. agenda ....

....

....

8. assets ....

....

....

9. affidavit ....

....

....

10. capital ....

....

....

WORK PROJECT 47

Mastering Business Terms: Cartel to Deed

A. Fill in the blank at the right with the number of the correct definition.

1. controller   ....
   1. the chief accountant in a large firm
   2. a corporation lawyer
   3. the head of the company security patrol

2. closed shop   ....
   1. a shop with all union employees
   2. a shop that is undergoing extensive repairs
   3. a shop that hires only men

3. consign   ....
   1. to sign as a witness
   2. to make a legal request
   3. to forward goods to another for their future sale

4. cartel   ....
   1. a shipping charge on breakable goods
   2. a clearinghouse of labor information
   3. an association of industrial firms that seeks to control prices or production of a specific item

5. debit   ....
   1. a large investment
   2. a debt
   3. a record of corporation taxes for a five-year period

B. Choose the word which fits the context and write it in the blank at the right.

1. The union spokesman argued that all employees should have the right of (consideration, collective bargaining, comparative advantage).   ....

2. The desperate rush to get out the monthly statements to customers could be avoided if we switched over to (data processing, cycle billing, conditional sale).   ....

3. Since most customers will make small purchases which they will want to take with them, I suggest we operate the business on a (cash-and-carry, carrying charge, cooperative) basis.   ....

4. It was specified in the (deed, contract, competition) that parking spaces for fifty automobiles were to be reserved for Plastite Company employees.

....

5. If you are unable or unwilling to do the merchandising yourself, why don't you locate a reliable (clientele, commission merchant, channel of distribution)?

....

6. A capitalistic society encourages (competition, consolidation, corporation) among businesses.

....

7. For a (consolidation, consideration, check-off) of $2,788 we will agree to design and build the patio at the Hibernia Bank building to be constructed at 108 Market Street.

....

8. Most appliances are purchased under the terms of a (consideration, channels of distribution, conditional sale) contract.

....

9. From now on the payroll department will specify the individual (balance of payments, check-offs, annuities) made against our monthly compensation.

....

10. The controller was instructed to prepare a financial report immediately after the annual (audit, check-off, closed shop).

....

WORK PROJECT 48

Mastering Business Terms:
Deficit to Itinerary

A.   Each business term in Column I would be most commonly used in an area described in Column II. In the blank at the right, place the letter of the area in Column II that corresponds to the business term in Column I.

	Column I		Column II		
1.	demurrage	A	operating expenses	1.	....
2.	deficit	B	money or money matters involved	2.	....
3.	depreciation	C	the volume of public buying	3.	....
4.	embargo	D	freight shipments	4.	....
5.	grievance	E	imports	5.	....
6.	elastic demand	F	loss of money	6.	....
7.	eminent domain	G	government spending	7.	....
8.	fixed cost	H	buildings and equipment	8.	....
9.	fiscal	I	labor-management relations	9.	....
10.	deficit financing	J	salaries	10.	....
11.	escalator clause	K	economic systems	11.	....
12.	depth interview	L	honesty and fairness in business dealings	12.	....
13.	free enterprise	M	hiring	13.	....
14.	good will	N	selfish concern	14.	....
15.	featherbedding	O	public use of property	15.	....

B.   In the space provided opposite each term, record the dictionary entry for syllabication and pronunciation (embargo: em bar' go). Then incorporate each term into a sentence of your own composing. If necessary, use the illustration in the glossary as a model.

1.   entrepreneur ....

....

....

....

2.   itinerary ....

....

....

3. demurrage ....

....

....

4. equity ....

....

....

5. escrow ....

....

....

6. deed ....

....

....

7. demurrage ....

....

....

8. data processing ....

....

....

9. inflation ....

....

....

10. good will ....

....

....

WORK PROJECT 49

**Mastering Business Terms:
Jobber to Net Worth**

A.   Some of the following terms are much more appropriate to one area of business than to another. List them under the proper headings. There will be at least one item for each heading. Do not place a term under more than one heading.

liquidity preference	margin
markup	markdown
merchandising	lien
liability	net sales
net cost	motivational research
national debt	liquidation
mediation	lockout
mortgage	

Buying stocks or securities

....

....

....

....

....

Personal, business, or governmental debt

....

....

....

....

....

Retail selling

....

....

....

....

....

Labor-management relations

....

....

....

....

....

Closing a business

....

....

....

....

....

B. In the space provided opposite each term, record the dictionary entry for the syllabication and pronunciation. Then incorporate each term into a sentence of your own composing. Use the illustration in the glossary as a model, if necessary.

1. laissez-faire ....

....

....

2. lien ....

....

....

3. negotiable ....

....

....

4. monopoly ....

....

....

5. liquidation ....

....

....

WORK PROJECT 50

Mastering Business Terms:
Night Letter to Wholesaler

A.   Fill in the blank at the right with the word in parentheses which is best identified by the explanation or description.

1. a device for advertising securities
    (night letter, prospectus, tickler)   ....

2. a period of decrease in wages and buying and of in-
    crease of unemployment
    (recession, reconciliation, sinking fund)   ....

3. the cost of operating a business
    (par value, overhead, sinking fund)   ....

4. a carefully conditioned public impression of a person
    or firm
    (speculation, seniority, public image)   ....

5. a related group of carefully planned shops with adja-
    cent parking area
    (trade association, shopping center, subsidiary com-
    panies)   ....

6. an assertion that a piece of merchandise is genuine
    (voucher, warranty, seal)   ....

7. a return on purchases, made to a member of a
    cooperative
    (patronage divided, parity price, vested interest)   ....

8. a person who passes goods from a producer to a
    retailer
    (stockholder, vendor, wholesaler)   ....

9. an earlier than anticipated loss of use of machinery
    or equipment
    (solvency, time and motion study, obsolescence)   ....

10. merchandising centered on one specific product or
    kind of goods
    (tariff, subsidy, specialty shop)   ....

B. Supply the missing term that suits the context and makes sense.

1. If you were the owner of a small retail store specializing in women's purses, you would call your store a ....

2. If you were able to pay all your legal debts, you could say that you were

....

3. If you were skeptical of the balance on your bank statement, you would go through the process called ....

4. If your brother were president of a company in which you held one thousand dollars in stock, you would have a .... in the affairs of that company.

5. If you were concerned to eliminate waste motions in some phase of an assembly line, you might hire someone to make a ....

6. If the form you were using had the ability to be transferred from one person to another, it would be ....

7. If you were figuring the actual cost of producing an item exclusive of expenses, you would speak of its ....

8. If some economic factor forced the retirement of equipment in your plant while it still had a useful life, you would call that fact ....

9. If you owned stock, the fixed value of each share would be known as the

....

10. If you gained a yield as a member of a cooperative, it could be called a

....